GW00708388

Housing Management, Community Care and Competitive Tendering

A Good Practice Guide

David Clapham and Bridget Franklin

Chartered Institute of Housing

The Chartered Institute of Housing

The Chartered Institute of Housing is the professional organisation for all people who work in housing. Its purpose is to take a strategic and leading role in encouraging and promoting the provision of good quality affordable housing for all. The Institute has more than 12,000 members working in local authorities, housing associations, the private sector and educational institutions.

Chartered Institute of Housing
Octavia House
Westwood Way
Coventry CV4 8JP
Telephone: 0203 694433

The *Joseph Rowntree Foundation* has supported this project as part of its programme of research and innovative development projects, which it hopes will be of value to policy makers and practitioners. The facts presented and views expressed in this report, however, are those of the authors and not necessarily those of the Foundation.

Housing Management, Community Care and Competitive Tendering
A Good Practice Guide

Authors: David Clapham and Bridget Franklin
Editor: John Perry

© Chartered Institute of Housing 1994
Published by the Chartered Institute of Housing

ISBN 0 901607 76 2

Graphic design by Henry's House Design Co–operative Ltd.
Printed by Warwick Printing Company Ltd.

Contents

About the Authors

David Clapham is Reader at the Centre for Housing Research and Urban Studies at the University of Glasgow.

Bridget Franklin is Research Fellow at the Centre for Housing Research and Urban Studies.

Acknowledgements

The authors would like to acknowledge the advice and assistance of the members of the Advisory Group for the project, established by the Joseph Rowntree Foundation who financed the research upon which this publication is based. Particular thanks are due to John Perry of the Chartered Institute of Housing and Ross Fraser of the Association of District Councils. Other members of the group were:

Peter Arnold, University of Humberside
Jane Brooke, Glasgow District Council
Tim Brown, St Helens MBC
Bill Puddicombe, New Era Housing Association Ltd
Peter Fletcher, Anchor Housing Association
Roger Howard, Roger Howard Associates
Christine Laird, Derby City Council
David Smith, Eastleigh Borough Council
Sandra Taylor, Nottinghamshire County Council
Jackie Wilkins, Joseph Rowntree Foundation
Pat Kneen, Joseph Rowntree Foundation

We also appreciate the assistance of Janet Richards of the Chartered Institute of Housing for comments on a draft version.

In addition, we would like to thank those local authority housing departments, social services (social work in Scotland) departments, housing associations and voluntary organisations which were willing to provide information, or to be included as case studies.

Finally, we express our thanks to Mary Coleman, Betty Johnstone and Tilly Wright for their patience in typing successive versions of this publication.

Introduction

What is the aim of the guide?

This guide is intended to help in the process of preparing for Compulsory Competitive Tendering (CCT) in local authority housing management. One of the crucial sets of decisions which has to be made concerns the aims and scope of housing management, which need to be reviewed in the light of the challenge which community care poses for housing management policies and practices. Therefore, the guide presents the potential role which housing management could play in community care and shows how this can be achieved in a CCT framework. The aim is to identify the key questions which those preparing for CCT will have to ask themselves as well as to offer practical guidance on implementing the chosen approach.

The guide is not intended to offer a detailed manual for the introduction of CCT. Those looking for this are referred to the joint ADC and IoH publication, *Competition and Local Authority Housing Services: a guidance manual (1993/4)*. Nor is the guide intended as a comprehensive statement of the role of housing in community care which covers a large number of issues including planning, needs assessment and supported accommodation. The focus is on the housing management service provided to tenants in ordinary tenancies although these other issues will be touched on briefly.

Who is the guide for?

The guide is intended primarily for housing managers in local authorities with strategic responsibilities for the implementation of CCT. However, it should also be of use to those charged with responsibility for more detailed tasks such as formulating the contract specification or devising measures to assess contract performance. Also, the guide should be useful to potential contractors for housing management services whether local authority housing departments or other agencies. Finally, agencies who are not preparing for CCT may still find the issues raised here of use to them in their efforts to provide an effective housing management service. In particular housing associations may find the issues raised here relevant in making decisions about the nature of their housing management services.

CCT and Housing Management

The main legislation governing CCT is contained within the 1988 Local Government Act, and was drafted in reference to services such as building maintenance, refuse collection and cleaning. This Act also contained a power for the government to extend CCT to other activities, a power which has been used to bring housing management and other white collar services within the legislation.

> '*The job of councils is to choose the best way of providing what people want. Some councils still patronise their tenants, apparently believing that only the council itself can provide the required service. But other authorities have shown that aspects of housing management can be performed best by those outside the council's employ. Compulsory competitive tendering will be introduced into the field of housing management.*'
> *Citizens White Paper,* Cmnd 1599, July 1991

The regulation and orders can be produced differently and separately in Scotland, but must in substance be the same as for England and Wales. Any variations must be justified by different circumstances.

What is singularly lacking in government guidelines is any attempt to address how either the social and welfare dimension of housing management or the extra requirements of those with community care needs can be catered for within the CCT process. Most authorities, and their representative bodies, are either not addressing these issues, or do not know how to do so. There is considerable concern over the ability of housing agencies to meet the increasing demands stemming from the housing of vulnerable people, within the CCT framework.

> *'There must be better ways of improving housing management nationally. CCT puts more value on money than people. But money should serve people, not the other way round.'*
> Peter Kegg, quoted by Morris 1994:9

> *'The commercial orientation sharpens the management perspective but conflicts with a service–based ethic.'*
> Walsh 1993

> *'I would say the sensitive treatment of rent collection, neighbour disputes and other parts of the service which are essentially about inter–personal relationships [are difficult to specify]. I am puzzled about how to specify in those cases so that you can control the outcome.'*
> Peter Mountford–Smith, quoted in *Housing*, July 1993:24

> *'Southwark has put forward the example of witness protection on housing estates where there have been arson attacks. How do you specify for that?*
> John Perry, quoted in *Housing*, July 1993:22

Interviews with case study authorities in the course of the research for this publication reveal the same unease:

> *'CCT isn't the best way to run a public service like housing which is a very sensitive one.'*
> Area Manager

> *'How to define the level of care that must be exercised is virtually impossible.'*
> Area Manager

> *'The whole rehousing question is so sensitive. We are not really comfortable with handing that over to the contractor, because we do not feel that there will be enough control over the caring side of it.'*
> Area Manager

> *'A troublesome tenant threatens managerial credibility as measured by performance criteria.'*
> Adult Services Manager, Social Services

> *'A housing officer may sit down and discuss with someone with a mental health problem how she is going to move, and then arrange transport for her – how do you put that in?'*
> Assistant Area Manager

CCT poses a considerable challenge to traditional ways of working in housing management and there is a large degree of scepticism amongst housing managers of the possibility of achieving social and welfare objectives within a CCT framework. The basic philosophy of this guide is that housing management has a crucial role to play in this respect and that it can and should continue this role under the joint challenges of CCT and community care. Suggestions are made for activities to be undertaken which are not usually included as part of the core housing management task, but which would be extremely beneficial in meeting particular difficulties faced by tenants with community care needs. However, the emphasis in the guide is on the similarity between tenants with community care needs and all those other tenants who are not perceived to fall into this category. In other words, effective and sensitive housing management benefits tenants with community care needs as much as it does all tenants. Therefore, the focus in this guide is mainly on the core housing management tasks which, when effectively performed, benefit all tenants. The guide endeavours to show that it is possible to specify for the continuance of a sensitive and responsive housing management service and that the present doubts displayed by some people may be unwarranted.

Definitions

> *'Community care means providing the services and support which people who are affected by problems of ageing, mental illness, mental handicap, or physical or sensory disability need to be able to live as independently as possible in their own homes, or in "homely" settings in the community'.*

> *Caring for People* Cmnd 849, 1989:3

It is important to make clear at the outset some key points which recur throughout the text. The government has defined community care narrowly to include people who are affected by problems of ageing, mental illness, mental handicap, or physical or sensory disability. However, many people who do not fall into these categories may have similar housing and support needs. Indeed, this is recognised in some government publications which have taken a much wider definition of those who come under the community care umbrella and many local authorities have also accepted that community care obligations extend to a much wider group. The focus in this guide will be on the provision of a housing management service for this wider group.

One authority's definition of community care groups:

- older people requiring support
- people with mental health problems
- people with learning difficulties
- people with physical disabilities, including wheelchair users and those with sensory impairment
- people with drug and alcohol related problems
- homeless young singles
- adult single homeless
- vulnerable single parents
- people with HIV
- ex–offenders
- refugees

The NHS and Community Care Act, 1990 set up specific procedures for dealing with community care. In particular, the procedures for the assessment of individual community care needs and the creation of a care package are important for housing management. People who have been involved in this process are referred to in the guide as *community care users*. However, not all tenants with support or care needs will have had an assessment. Therefore, the term *tenants with community care needs* will be used as a general term to cover all tenants with these needs whatever administrative label these people are given or procedural route they follow.

The Research

The information used in this guide has been collected as part of a research project on community care, housing management and CCT carried out by the authors and funded by the Joseph Rowntree Foundation. The research focused on six local authorities and two housing associations and examined their approaches to community care issues. Interviews were held with housing management staff at all levels and with relevant social services personnel to ascertain their views on the contribution of housing management to community care. As part of the interviews a number of vignettes or fictitious case examples were shown to staff to find out how they would react in particular circumstances and what their expectations of other professionals were. The quotations used in this guide are taken from these interviews.

One of the six local authorities was a CCT pilot authority. In addition, information was gathered from another pilot authority although this was not considered in the same depth as the other six local authorities.

Outline

Chapter 1 starts by outlining the general role of housing in community care, before focusing on the potential role of housing management in providing housing and support for tenants with community care needs. The emphasis is on providing options for those preparing for CCT to consider in making vital decisions on the kind of service they require.

Chapter 2 focuses on the review of the housing management service which is necessary in preparation for CCT and emphasises the community care issues which need to be considered and the decisions which have to be taken.

Chapter 3 examines the issues which need to be addressed in drawing up the contract. The general framework of the contract documentation is discussed with particular emphasis on provisions for tenants with community care needs.

Chapter 4 looks at the central task of designing the contract specification for CCT. The chapter also offers detailed examples of how to include housing management tasks crucial to community care in the specification for particular housing management activities.

Chapter 5 considers the approach of two CCT pilot authorities and draws out certain key issues which might assist other authorities in their own preparations for CCT.

The *conclusion* draws together the main decisions which need to be taken if an effective, community care oriented housing management service is to be achieved through the CCT process.

Chapter 1
Housing Management and Community Care

The aim of this chapter is to discuss the contribution which housing management can make to the achievement of community care aims. The chapter starts with a review of the general role of housing in community care. Issues such as the involvement of housing agencies in community care planning could influence the potential contribution that housing management can make to community care.

The focus will be on how the scope and content of housing management is defined and the factors which influence that definition. The key question is whether the emphasis should be on housing management as a commercial business or as a social service. In the present climate it has to be a mixture of both and later chapters aim to give some guidance on how they can be reconciled.

The chapter continues with an analysis of the potential role of housing management in community care, looking at the different kinds of activities involved and the questions surrounding their implementation.

The Role of Housing in Community Care

It has been widely acknowledged in government statements that housing is the cornerstone of community care. The philosophy of normalisation which underpins much community care provision emphasises the aims of integration and of keeping people in socially valued environments such as ordinary housing or in homely settings such as small scale, supported accommodation projects. In practice it seems that housing issues have not been fully integrated into the community care agenda and housing agencies have felt themselves at the margins of community care policy making. There are a number of areas where housing can make a contribution to community care.

i)   *Housing in Community Care Planning*

Social services departments have a statutory duty to produce an annual community care plan outlining needs in their area and their plans to meet this need. There is a statutory duty to consult others such as housing and health agencies, users and the private sector. Health and housing agencies still produce their own plans.

Community care plans are meant to contain an assessment of needs, a statement of priorities, and targets, programmes and policies by which they are to be achieved. Housing needs and the availability of housing accommodation to meet them should be key elements of the community care plan.

Attention has largely focused on the liaison arrangements to bring housing into the planning process. It is suggested that a structure such as a housing forum should be established in each area to bring together housing organisations and put them in touch with health and social services agencies (Scottish Office, 1994). Working groups can be established from time to time to review policies on particular issues or for particular groups. Information on good practice in this area is given in Arnold et al (1993) and in the *Housing Management Standards Manual* produced by the Chartered Institute of Housing.

A further issue is exactly what housing agencies have to offer to the community care planning process. In the past, planning for supported accommodation has all too often been based solely on the unthinking application of crude targets, for example so many sheltered housing places per thousand older people. Information to ensure greater accuracy can be gleaned from a variety of sources such as the assessment process itself, and there needs to be substantial investment in the management information systems which are required to make use of these sources. The emphasis on ordinary housing implicit in normalisation means that planning must also be concerned with the availability of mainstream accommodation. Guidance on an appropriate method of assessing need is given in *Community Care Planning: a model for housing needs assessment* by Watson and Harker (1993). The Institute is planning further work in this area.

Also, there is a need to integrate community care planning with the housing planning process to ensure that community care needs are taken into account in the housing strategy and vice versa.

Crucially the community care planning process offers an opportunity for housing agencies to achieve good working relations with social services, health and other agencies involved in the provision of community care services. It provides a forum for understanding the policies, priorities and objectives of these agencies and of reaching an agreement on common principles. Overlaps and gaps in the provision of services can be identified and action taken to deal with them. Clarity can be achieved in the boundaries of organisational responsibility and procedures worked out for liaison on individual issues and cases.

Liaison arrangements are crucial at all levels if the community care needs of tenants are to be met effectively. The purchaser–provider split in both housing and social services makes liaison arrangements more complex but no less vital. If communication with other agencies is good, then many problems with the CCT process may be avoided as their understanding and co–operation will be vital at many stages. Therefore, a review of existing liaison arrangements and the establishment of effective arrangements at all levels is an important first step in preparing for CCT.

In practice the relationships between housing and health and social services agencies are often poor, although there are exceptions. Often relations with one agency are good but are poor with others. Much seems to depend on local priorities and the individuals involved.

There is clearly a lot of misunderstanding between housing and social services agencies about their respective roles. In general, housing officers feel that social services are not doing their job and they are incorrectly being asked to fill the gaps. However, social workers argue that their priorities do not always accord with what housing think they should be and that housing are asking for the impossible.

> '*Housing takes the view that anyone with a problem needs a social worker – this is not possible given social work priorities. In*

*addition, there can't be an open–ended relationship with clients,
involvement will always be limited.'*
Social Worker

In general, social services professionals think that housing officers
should be carrying out more of a socially oriented role: 'the human face
of housing should be there'. However, it is recognised that there should
be limits to their activity.

> *'Housing workers should be looking only at whether someone can
> manage a tenancy and a house. They are not competent to identify
> and deal with social issues, although individuals vary in their
> ability to do this.'*
> Social Worker

ii)   *Assessment*

The most important element of the new system implemented from
April 1993 is individual community care needs assessments which are to
be given to every person who asks for one, or on whose behalf one is
requested. The legislation has resulted in social services agencies
reviewing their existing assessment processes and instituting formal and
systematic assessment procedures. Some assessments may be
straightforward – every person requesting a home help will not
necessarily have to undergo a complex assessment procedure before
receiving the service.

An elderly person leaving hospital may or may not have a community
care assessment, depending on the circumstances, but would almost
certainly do so if one of the options under consideration was to enter a
residential home. A person who is not able to cope in his or her own
home, particularly if there was a possibility of institutionalisation, is also
likely to have a care assessment. The purpose of this is to establish
whether giving up the home is the most appropriate option, or whether
additional support to the person, or adaptations or improvements to the
home, might enable the person to remain. In theory people leaving a
psychiatric hospital will undergo an assessment and have a 'key worker'
assigned to them, usually a social worker or a community psychiatric
nurse, who will take responsibility for co–ordinating their care plan and

providing support for a definite or indefinite period. Care plans are to be reviewed every three months.

There are many people with special needs who are only potential community care clients. They may live in the community entirely unsupported, or with input from statutory or voluntary agencies, carers, relatives, friends or neighbours. Some may be identified by themselves or others as having a need for an assessment in order to gain the support they feel is needed. If approached, a social worker may not agree that there is a need. Some authorities may also have a system for classifying cases as of high, medium or low priority, with those of low priority waiting months, if not years, for an assessment.

> '*When it comes to co–operation with social services I think our housing officers' general view is that they don't get as much co–operation as they would like, because whenever the housing officer thinks they have got a social services case social services will say, no, it isn't a potential case, it isn't severe enough.*'
> Area Manager

According to central government guidelines, assessments are to be driven by the needs of the person being assessed who has to be given a written needs assessment. There is a statutory duty to consult housing authorities in relation to assessments. The aim of assessment is to produce a care package to meet the identified needs and it is inevitable that resources will not be available to meet all assessed needs. There has already been some controversy over this issue, because an authority not meeting assessed need could lay itself open to legal challenge for being in breach of its statutory duties. For this reason it seems likely that needs assessments will be influenced by the resources available, although it is unclear by how much.

It seems in most cases that assessments are being carried out by staff of social services departments with housing only being contacted if there is considered to be an important housing dimension. This raises the question of the ability of assessors to recognise housing need. It is essential that sufficient information on housing is gained in the assessment process and the assessor needs to have the skill and experience to interpret it so that housing involvement can be triggered where necessary. Knowledge of housing options by an assessor is important because there is a degree of interchangeability between some support and housing needs. For example, the need for support may be met through a move of house closer to family carers. There is a question of whether housing staff should be involved directly in all or a proportion of assessments and whether resources exist for housing agencies to undertake this role. At present housing staff are often being expected to make allocation decisions on the basis of partial information, which may require further substantiation through informal contacts.

It is important that the criteria used in the assessment process are co–ordinated with those used by housing agencies in allocating both mainstream tenancies and places in supported accommodation. Any discrepancy could cause confusion and delay to users. Therefore, liaison arrangements should be used to establish agreed criteria which can be universally applied.

A vital prerequisite for the CCT process is agreement over the involvement of the housing agency in the assessment process. It is crucial that housing expertise and the views of the housing agency are available when decisions over individual needs are being made and care packages assembled. Housing agencies need to review the implications of agreed assessment criteria for their housing management services, particularly allocation policies, procedures and priorities. However, assessment decisions on, for example, whether a person is capable of independent living could have profound implications for all features of the housing management service.

iii)   *Supported Accommodation*

A major role of housing agencies in community care will be planning, developing and helping to run supported accommodation schemes, often in partnership with a voluntary organisation or the social services department or health agencies. There is a long history of such schemes and substantial experience has been gained by housing agencies which can be built on. Examples of good practice in this area are provided in the Institute's *Housing Management Standards Manual*.

However, it seems likely that the present emphasis on supported accommodation may not be sustained. The objective of normalisation stresses the need for integration and for as normal an environment as possible which can best be achieved in ordinary housing. The costs of developing new supported accommodation projects, the growth of the numbers of community care users, especially older people, and growing realisation of the drawbacks of supported accommodation may mean that people will be more likely to be supported in ordinary housing.

The drawbacks of supported accommodation are the inflexibility associated with the tying together of housing and support. This can mean that people may have to move into supported accommodation from their own home in order to gain support (for example, an older person moving into a sheltered or very sheltered scheme because of poor health) or alternatively may have to move from the scheme if their support needs change.

Countries such as Denmark, Canada and Australia are attempting to deal with the problems of supported accommodation by separating the delivery of housing and care services. The philosophy is that no–one should have to move in order to receive care. Housing and care are considered to be linked but separate. Care is closely targeted in order to meet the individual needs of users whether someone is in their own home, supported accommodation or residential care. The emphasis is on flexibility, with care not being tied closely in a rigid package to particular residential locations.

Nevertheless, there will clearly still be a major role for supported accommodation and the experience and expertise of housing agencies will be vital. It will be necessary for housing agencies to review their policies on supported accommodation and to reach an agreed view with other agencies on its role and the criteria used in deciding who should be housed in it. This is needed to ensure that allocation priorities accord with decisions taken in the assessment process and that the implications for the management service in mainstream tenancies are understood.

iv)   *Housing Management*

Government policy is undoubtedly leading to more users of community care living in their own homes, often in public sector housing. Any move away from supported accommodation in the future will reinforce this trend. Current domiciliary services are not sufficient to provide all the support that may be needed in these circumstances and there has been increasing pressure from tenants and from other agencies for housing management to fill some of the gaps. Also, among some housing agencies there has been a growing awareness of the potential of housing–based services to contribute strongly and positively to successful community care. Therefore, there is a need for agencies preparing for CCT to review their existing housing management practices and assess their relevance to tenants with community care needs.

Housing Management and Community Care

'I believe a housing officer should be managing their estates, and that means by inference, managing or helping the tenants on those estates. There isn't time for a housing officer to visit everybody on a regular basis but they should be out on the estate as much as possible. If passing people you know have special problems you should be calling in to see how they are and to see if you can help with anything. This would include noting if they were coping physically and mentally. Also, if a workman mentioned he thought there was a problem a housing officer should go and check. It's not in the job description to be looking into whether someone is occupying their time but you could make suggestions. I used to call in on a lunch club to take any repairs, and to see if there were any problems or anyone was missing. But I think there comes a point where a housing officer cannot be expected to meet the special needs of those people.'
Assistant Area Housing Manager

There has never been a clear, generally accepted definition of what housing management is, and practice has varied considerably over time. Today, local authorities are under pressure from two directions which at first seem to be incompatible. On the one hand there is pressure from tenants, from other agencies and from the perceived self–interest of landlords to adopt a socially oriented role. On the other hand there is pressure from central government in particular to adopt a more commercial approach.

Definitions of what constitutes the social role of housing management vary. The Institute has defined it as consisting of the following tasks:

• debt counselling and benefits advice

- racial harassment prevention
- dealing with effects of alcohol and drug abuse
- liaison with social services over community care, children at risk or the mentally ill
- dealing with environmental problems such as dogs, traffic or litter
- helping to develop community projects such as play schemes or 'good neighbour' schemes
- arranging adaptations for people with disabilities
- wider aspects of neighbour disputes
- working with police to improve security or deal with anti–social behaviour
- welfare aspects of wardens' work
- supported accommodation
- community alarms
- community development (newsletters, residents' meetings)

Those who consider housing management should be confined to tasks which concern only the 'bricks and mortar' landlord function may dispute the relevance of much in this list. However, amongst others there is a perception that there is an increasing need to take on some form of social role. The relative pressures of the social role and the commercial role will now be considered in turn.

i)   *Pressures for the Social Role*

> *'It's unfortunate really that we are judged on arrears and voids and really it's not about that any more. That's part of the job but a lot of it is the social side of the job... You can't just turn your back on people now, and say pay your rent or else. I don't believe it's housing's job to be a carer, although it is a big part of our job. You can't just turn round and say "well I'm not going to do that... you've got to assess the situation".'*
> Housing Officer

One of the factors which is leading to a more socially oriented role is community care, which has resulted in people who previously would have been in institutions or supported accommodation living in mainstream tenancies. As a consequence housing managers are providing a service to tenants who are or should be in contact with many welfare services such as social security, social work, health or education. The needs of tenants are not neatly compartmentalised into organisationally or professionally defined areas and so inevitably there is pressure for housing managers to become involved in a range of issues. The residualisation of council housing has had a similar, although perhaps stronger impact. Council (and to a lesser extent housing association) housing is being increasingly confined to the most vulnerable people in society. Through policies such as the Right–to–Buy, those who are able to afford to become owner–occupiers are doing so. As a result council housing is increasingly becoming a tenure of last resort. The economic problems of the 1980s and 1990s and growing inequality have compounded these problems. The nature of council housing itself, sometimes built in large estates on the edge of towns and cities, has contributed to the isolation and social stigma which social and economic policies have created. Housing agencies have often taken a pivotal role in attempts by a wide range of agencies to alleviate the problems of such areas.

Therefore, pressures for a more socially oriented role in housing management are not confined to community care. Nevertheless, decisions on the objectives and scope of housing management need to be taken in the light of community care needs and their relationship to other important social needs.

> '*Housing officers are human beings, if they saw a problem in a property they would be expected to deal with it on a human level. We expect to offer a caring service.*'
> Area Manager

Some of the pressure to adopt a social role has arisen because of social services priorities. There is clearly a lot of misunderstanding between housing and social services agencies about their respective roles and this has led to disputes about who should be doing what, and pressure on housing agencies to fill some of the gaps in current provision.

ii)   *Pressures for the 'Commercial' Role*

There are two main factors which seem to be pushing local authorities away from a socially oriented role and towards a more commercial approach. The first is the implications of the *Ealing judgement* and the second is CCT.

The key point from the *Ealing judgement* is that it seems to have lent weight to existing pressures to limit the extent of the activities which can be charged to the Housing Revenue Account (HRA). The principle accepted by the judges in the case was that activities charged to the HRA should be ones carried out for all tenants and not just a subset (the particular issue in the judgement was the cost of sheltered housing wardens' salaries). The judgement had obvious attractions to a government committed to reductions in public expenditure because of the potential it offered for the reduction of housing benefit expenditure. However, the government was persuaded that any rapid change would create chaos and that it was important not to threaten the social role of housing management by insisting that such activities be financed from the general fund. At present the long–term situation is unclear, although immediate threats to the social role seem to have receded considerably.

The second major factor is CCT which will be dealt with in detail in subsequent chapters. The concern over CCT is that it will lead to pressures to keep costs down in order to be competitive, perhaps leading to reluctance to be involved in activities associated with the social role which may be perceived to be peripheral to the main tasks of collecting rent, carrying out repairs and so on. Even if there is a desire to include social activities it is commonly felt that they are difficult to specify and measure and therefore to include in a CCT contract. This point will be dealt with fully in the following chapters.

Statutory performance indicators have been laid down for local authorities to produce each year which cover the core activities of housing management rather than any social role. Therefore, the message to local authorities from central government seems to be to concentrate on the basics.

> *'We would like to be able to do more than provide a roof over someone's head but neither the time nor the resources are available to offer the necessary support. Problems lie in the lack of resources and the government's concern to measure things in tables rather than any concern for a caring service.'*
> Area Manager

Arguments For The Social Role
- meets the wide–ranging needs of tenants
- increases tenant satisfaction

- is the duty of local authorities as the providers of public services
- is in the interests of landlords because it increases the likelihood of tenancies being maintained thus leading to lower voids
- can prevent or reduce problems of rent arrears, vandalism and neighbour disputes which may be associated with the breakdown of tenancies
- will contribute towards inter–agency approaches to regenerate disadvantaged areas.

Arguments Against The Social Role
- housing officers do not have the appropriate skills and knowledge
- treading on other agencies' toes
- is expensive in terms of staff time
- distracts attention from the basics of housing management
- creates stigma by becoming a social service
- re–inforces trends towards residualisation
- is difficult to implement in the current climate of performance measurement and CCT.

Every housing agency needs to decide whether it wants to adopt a social role. The view of the Institute is that the social role is fundamental and expresses the true nature of the housing management task.

> *'The Institute believes that services of this kind are important elements of the landlord role. These services are an integral part of social housing management, and are the characteristics which distinguish it from "bricks and mortar" property management.'*
> Institute of Housing, April 1993

It is our view that the arguments against adoption of the social role do not stand up to scrutiny. If housing managers do not have appropriate skills they should receive training to acquire them. Far from treading on the toes of other agencies and professionals, the social role entails working with them more closely and identifying overlaps and gaps to be filled. There is also a strong argument that the time and resources devoted to the role in the short term will pay off in the longer term with lower void rates, less vandalism, lower rent arrears and so on. Therefore, the social role does not distract from the basics of housing management, but plays a vital part in achieving objectives in this area. Adopting a social role does not increase the problems of residualisation, but is vital if the problems are to be confronted. Current trends have gone too far to be ignored in the vain hope that council housing will become a large, general needs tenure in the near future. The only route open is to adapt to meet the new circumstances. Finally, we hope to show in the rest of this study how the social role as it relates to community care can be achieved within the framework of CCT.

Defining the Community Care Role

'There should be the ability to cross over the narrow job definition as it means more continuity and understanding for the client. Housing managers should have a role in the identification of need and monitoring of people in the community, similar to a key worker role. They should be able to recognise situations where there is a community care need and be initiators of that process. They should collaborate in the process of the assessment of care as well as housing then they understand what is involved and can take part in monitoring. They are in a position to keep the threads of a package of care together and act as an information point.'
Community Care Planning Officer

In preparation for CCT decisions have to be made about the scope of the housing management service considered appropriate in order to meet community care needs. There is a core of tasks which need to be carried out for all tenants such as core housing management, housing advice and community support, with intensive housing management for the vulnerable tenants who need it, some but not all of whom will be tenants with community care needs.

The obvious point to make about the core activities is that they are as important to tenants with community care needs as they are to other tenants. Further, it could be argued that they are more important because those with community care needs may be more vulnerable than tenants as a whole and may be more tied to the home and its environs because of mobility problems. A person with recurrent mental illness does not want to have extra anxiety caused by a repair not being satisfactorily carried out or by living in a threatening environment

The first duty of a public landlord towards people with community care needs is to provide a good quality housing management service.

The second duty is to provide it in a way which is sensitive to their particular needs.

There is considerable guidance on the provision of a good housing management service, for example, in the Institute's *Housing Management Standards Manual*. We give some examples in the following chapters of how to provide a sensitive service within the framework of CCT.

However, this basic service, even if provided efficiently and effectively may mean that there are gaps in provision for meeting the community care needs of tenants. Therefore, it is necessary to review provision in collaboration with social services and health to reach agreement on whose responsibility it is to provide those support activities which form part of the social role and how they should be financed. It must be recognised that there are costs associated with these activities although they may be offset by savings in terms of lower void rates and so on.

The range of activities identified by the Institute as making up the social role is somewhat diffuse. In making decisions with regard to community care it may be helpful to group activities into categories as follows:

• Core Housing Management Tasks
• Intensive Housing Management
• Housing Advice and Information/Community Care Assessments
• Community Support
• Brokerage Tasks
• Practical, Non–Personal, Dwelling Related Support
• Practical, Non–Personal, Non–Dwelling Related Tasks
• Practical Personal Support or 'Care' Tasks
• Physical Health Services
• Emotional Support

Core Housing Management Tasks
These are the basic landlord functions which have to be carried out by all landlords to all tenants in order for the landlord/tenant relationship to function, and include organising repairs, collecting rents, making allocations and enforcing tenancy conditions.

Intensive Housing Management
These are the tasks as above, but they may have to be carried out more intensively for tenants with particular problems such as community care

needs. Examples may be the need for more guidance on the terms and conditions of tenancy, and initial welfare benefits information.

Core and intensive housing management are clearly housing tasks and it could be argued that landlords would be failing in their duty if they did not carry them out.

Housing Advice and Information/Community Care Assessments
Although general housing advice and information may be perceived as part of the core management tasks there are particular issues for community care groups. For example, advice for those considering whether to move on or stay put, discussion of options, adaptations, possibility of moving closer to a carer etc. This could extend to taking part in community care assessments. The provision of more detailed advice on housing and other welfare benefits may also come into this category.

Housing advice and information is considered to be primarily a housing responsibility as only housing staff have the relevant information and expertise to offer appropriate advice. However, the task is sometimes not undertaken by housing departments and is either not done at all or is undertaken by independent organisations or social work staff.

Community Support
This concerns the provision of services, advice and support to ensure that the community functions in an effective way. Included are the promotion of tenants' groups and other community organisations, involvement in crime prevention schemes, estate regeneration initiatives and so on. Such activities benefit all tenants in an area including perhaps especially users of community care.

Community support has become a crucial part of what is considered to be good practice in housing. Arrangements for tenant participation have increased considerably in recent years and much more financial and other support is offered to tenants' groups. In addition, housing staff are often involved in multi–agency efforts to regenerate particular communities.

Brokerage Tasks
These are intended to ensure that tenants receive services from other agencies such as social services, gas companies and so on. It may involve acting as an advocate for tenants with these agencies.

Brokerage is a task which does not require particular professional skills. Common–sense, basic information about the responsibilities of different agencies and office equipment and time are all that is required. Brokerage may involve trying to get water re–connected, liaising with the DSS over a benefit claim, contacting the social services department to ask for a home help service and so on. It involves keeping an eye on tenants and being able to assess the help required.

In some housing offices brokerage is frequently undertaken, but in others it is considered to be a social services responsibility. Practice varies sometimes between different offices in the same local authority and sometimes between individual housing officers. In one authority in our research there was an implicit agreement that social services undertook brokerage for families and housing undertook it for single people.

Brokerage tasks can be successfully carried out by housing or social services or conceivably by an independent agency. The most important points are that they should be carried out by *somebody* and the needs of community care users not ignored, and that there is an explicit agreement about who does what to avoid overlaps and gaps.

Practical, Non–Personal, Dwelling Related Support

Practical, non–personal, dwelling related support is a long–winded title for a category of tasks which are sometimes carried out by housing departments, but often not on a consistent basis. The most common tasks are internal decoration, the provision of furniture, and help with gardening, sometimes by arrangement with a voluntary organisation. They tend to be carried out on a one–off basis, at the beginning of a tenancy or in a crisis, and are usually discretionary. There is sometimes a special budgetary allocation for the tasks. Again there can be overlap with social services departments who may provide help with purchasing furniture and so on.

There is another set of tasks which are often not carried out at all and fall between housing and social services. Examples are heavy (spring) cleaning, changing a fuse or a light bulb, moving heavy furniture and so on. These tasks are not usually undertaken by home helps, nor do they count as repairs. The tasks are relatively small but can be of great importance to tenants. There is potential for housing departments to undertake these tasks and therefore to make a substantial contribution to meeting community care needs.

Practical, Non–Personal, Non–Dwelling Related Tasks

There are problems for housing managers in deciding whether to undertake practical non–personal, non–dwelling related tasks. The key is the definition of non–dwelling related. As one housing manager said.

'A trigger for action appears to be if there is a problem which is affecting other people, the housing department income, or the property in some way. These factors would lead housing to be involved in what would be some sort of support/social role.'

The problem is knowing where to draw the boundary because of the wide range of factors which could influence the ability of a tenant to sustain successfully a tenancy. For example, should housing agencies be involved in home–maker schemes which aim to give tenants the skills to be able to live independently and sustain a tenancy? Other non–dwelling related services such as shopping or preparing food are occasionally carried out in an emergency by some housing staff such as concierges, but this is relatively unusual. In most cases these are left to the home help service. Nevertheless, there can be a real dilemma for housing officers who are aware of unmet need which could threaten a tenancy.

Practical Personal Support or 'Care' Tasks

This includes for example help with bathing or getting in or out of bed. An alternative title could be personal attendance functions.

Practical personal support is not usually carried out by housing staff, although in our research we found one or two examples of staff with appropriate training undertaking these tasks in emergency situations where no–one else was available. However, no–one argued that this should be anything other than a very rare occurrence.

Physical Health Services and Emotional Support

These involve assessing health, checking on or administering medication and evaluating or promoting a person's emotional health. In practice it can be difficult to distinguish the latter activity from befriending.

In this categorisation it can be argued that physical health services, and the fostering of emotional support are the responsibility of health and social services. Indeed it could be dangerous for staff without appropriate medical or social work skills and knowledge to become involved.

In our research we came across some examples of housing staff becoming involved in these activities, but this was usually when they had previously been trained and employed as a social worker or a psychiatric nurse. Housing staff with no special background sometimes befriended tenants, providing advice and support, listening and giving sympathy. They usually did this from a personal liking for the tenant and a desire to help. This help is usually highly appreciated by tenants and would seem to be useful as long as staff are trained to recognise when professional help is required.

Organising for Housing Management in Community Care

In the last 20 years the housing service has followed the trends of decentralisation and genericism. However, there seems to be something of a backlash against both of these trends in recent years with a few housing departments moving in the opposite direction.

Community care poses new problems to be considered in deciding on the appropriate scale and organisation of housing management. The key issue of the degree of specialism as opposed to genericism is entangled in choice of the appropriate scale of housing management for community care. Are community care issues best dealt with by specialists or by generic housing offices or by a combination of both? The argument for **genericism** is as follows:

- sensitivity to community care needs in everyday housing management
- a more seamless service
- greater knowledge of context of local area
- equality of treatment for community care users leading to less stigma
- a more locally–based service
- local links with other agencies
- less danger of duplicating services with other agencies

The argument for **specialism** is:

- more knowledge and experience of the needs of community care users and ways of dealing with them
- concentration of expertise and training on a few staff
- less danger of community care needs being forgotten
- avoids conflicts with demands for other housing management tasks to take precedence

The advantages outlined are not proven to exist and may depend on local circumstances. Basically, the case for community care needs to be met within generic housing management is that needs can be met in an integrated way in a local setting without involving other housing staff. The problem is that all staff will require some training in community care if they are to recognise needs and be able to deal appropriately with them.

> *'All right you have got certain knowledge of social care, but to get involved in something that you're not trained in can be dicey ground.'*
> Housing Officer

Even if training is provided, each housing officer may still only meet a tenant with mental health problems every few years. There is therefore no opportunity to build up expertise and there may be a danger of staff getting out of their depth. Also, there may be pressure to overlook or neglect the community care role in the concern for basis housing management targets.

The case for specialisation is based on the ability to concentrate expertise in a few staff. The success of this strategy will depend on factors such as referral procedures by estate–based staff and communication between the two. Inevitably there will be liaison difficulties and specialist staff may lack knowledge of local conditions.

The choice of strategy to adopt may be influenced by the approach to CCT. Where the minimum service is being contracted out, community care specialist staff may be able to stay with the client side organisation. Where a wider range of services are contracted out a generic strategy may be easier. Choice will also depend on the extent to which community care activities are to be undertaken. If brokerage and practical support are not offered then the scope for specialist staff is reduced.

Checklist: Housing Management and Community Care

☑ Have you reviewed existing liaison arrangements at all levels with social services and health authorities and taken steps to improve them where necessary?

☑ Have you agreed the nature and timing of the housing input into the community care plan?

☑ Have you agreed with the other agencies a procedure to be involved in community care assessments in an effective and appropriate way?

☑ Have you reviewed allocations and other housing management policies in the light of criteria used in the assessment process?

☑ Do you have an agreed policy for supported accommodation and a clear understanding of who it is meant for and the procedures for assessing need?

☑ Have you reviewed housing management policies, procedures and priorities in the light of community care needs?

☑ Have you identified some potentially new ways housing management services could be expanded to fill unmet community care needs?

☑ Do you have a clear and agreed policy on the scope of housing management and its relationship to the provision of other agencies?

Some Examples

There are many examples where housing agencies undertake some of the tasks listed above in a constructive and innovative way which is appreciated by tenants with community care needs. Some of those described come from floating support schemes or supported accommodation, but there is no reason why they cannot in principle be adopted as standard practice in the management of mainstream tenancies. The examples quoted often 'pick and mix' activities from the different categories outlined earlier and so do not always offer clear–cut examples of choosing to undertake a complete category of activities.

27

The examples are meant to stimulate ideas and to suggest activities which could be undertaken as part of a positive community care contribution. Other examples are given in the Institute's *Housing Management Standards Manual*.

....

Example 1

A Concierge Scheme

Concierges have been introduced into a number of high rise blocks in a large urban local authority in an attempt to improve security and reduce lettings and voids problems. Concierges work in teams of 11, and provide a 24 hour staffed reception desk with closed circuit television to scan public areas both inside and outside the block.

The duties of concierges are stated as cleaning, reception, security and welfare. The job description is deliberately fairly unspecific to allow scope for initiative. The concierges themselves see cleaning and security as secondary to what they perceive as the helping role. They are not involved in the allocations process but do accompanied viewing, welcome and show round new tenants. They can provide benefit forms etc but only offer limited help in filling them in. Any queries are noted for the next visit of the housing officer. All the tenants are known to them, often by christian name, and if someone has not been observed for a few days the concierges will check if they are all right.

Concierges play an important part in neighbour disputes, and try to resolve them before reporting to the housing officer. They also act as a point of contact ('a great go–between') for other services – police, G.P., social workers, hospital etc, although on the whole this is to take and pass on messages rather than making judgements about a case. Any actual liaison is done by the housing officer, which the concierges see as a reflection of the view that is taken of them as manual workers.

The concierges pride themselves on doing more or less anything they are asked eg:

- giving early morning calls
- taking in people's keys when they go out
- making cups of tea for those using the laundry

- talking to lonely individuals on the phone or at the desk
- changing light bulbs
- fitting or replacing plugs
- opening jars
- moving heavy items
- putting up curtains
- cleaning landings for elderly/disabled
- dressing wounds
- 'doing the carrots'

Concierges do not hoover or shop, although they have on occasion fetched a prescription. They are alert to those who are elderly or vulnerable in some way, and would for instance check that such a person has a fire on in cold weather. They have been known to cook a meal for a tenant in an emergency. In some cases they get quite involved with individual tenants, for example calming a man with emotional and drink problems who has regular panic attacks, dealing with a woman with mental health problems who should have had a community care assessment months ago, helping a deaf and dumb woman with a disturbed personality.

Concierges feel they exceed the scope of what they should strictly be doing, but on the other hand it is these aspects of the job that give the most satisfaction. They see themselves as providing 'a front line day–to–day service', and as a 'good friend' of the housing officer. There is no conflict between the respective jobs, even though some of the previously exclusive preserve of the housing officer has been taken over by the concierge.

....

....

Example 2

A Floating Support Scheme

A floating support scheme run by one London–based specialist Housing Association offers permanent tenancies in self–contained flats to individuals who are referred as having 'low support needs'. The accommodation is permanent and not part of a 'move–on' process. The service provided is described as one of Housing Management; the housing officer will not be expected to deal with the personal affairs of the tenants.

Contact is responsive, dependent upon housing management issues such as problems in rent payment/computer records, arrears, feeding back any housing benefit delays, inspecting repairs and tenancy issues. However, it is envisaged that more staff input may be required during the initial few weeks of a tenancy. During this period more detailed work may involve contact with DSS, Housing Benefit, the connection of gas, electricity and water supply. Emphasis will be on enabling the tenant to deal with these aspects independently.

Any work done on budgeting or money management will be from a housing management perspective, therefore should the tenant express a requirement for more detailed help, a referral may be made to an appropriate agency.

An information pack will be compiled giving information on the area, including local facilities, GP's in the area, education, job centres, advice agencies, along with details of the housing association's policies.

The housing officer may, from time to time be required to liaise with external agencies such as local social services or community psychiatric nurses. Referrals may be made to agencies offering counselling, specialist support/advice or specific training should it be appropriate.

A support plan will be drawn up with tenants prior to their move. This will be subject to regular review with the eventual aim of withdrawing the additional support.

The support plan is intended to be an individual plan, the frequency of meetings will depend upon the requirements identified. However, during the initial three months the housing worker and tenant will meet at least monthly.

A meeting will be arranged with the prospective tenant prior to the tenancy being signed. At this meeting practical requirements will be identified, such as: applying for Benefit, changing address of Benefit Office, arranging for services to be connected, purchase/delivery of furniture. This may include several other appointments being made.

Following the initial interview a draft support plan will be drawn up which will be discussed and possibly amended at this meeting. This will involve identification of any longer term requirements and appropriate action will be agreed.

It may be useful to have the key worker from the referring agency at this meeting.

The support plan will form part of the Tenancy Agreement. A new tenancy will be signed when the floating support is withdrawn and the property moves into the general needs section.

....

....

Example 3

Job Description of Support Worker in a Housing Association Project for Single Homeless People

1 To assist tenants in claiming entitlement to benefits and maximise income, liaising with relevant statutory authorities.

2 To offer help and advice on budgeting, advising on fuel debt and liaising with fuel boards.

3 To ensure the involvement of statutory and voluntary organisations if required, eg Social Services, charities, liaising closely with such organisations.

4 To offer a befriending service to tenants, providing a confidential/counselling service.

5 To liaise between tenants and deal with disputes.

6 To supervise use of communal facilities, ie communal lounge and laundry.

7 To encourage self–help by helping to organise a tenants association (with assistance from the Association's Tenant Participation Worker).

8 To arrange help in areas such as decorating, draught–proofing, meals on wheels, etc, in respect of more vulnerable tenants.

9 The association will arrange rent collection systems. The Support Worker will be aware of methods and will be kept advised of payments and arrears and will assist the Association with collection.

10 The Support Worker will report repairs to the Association and will arrange access for contractors.

11 The Support Worker will notify the Association immediately of vacancies, and will assist new tenants to settle into the project (allocations will be made by the Association).

12 The Support Worker will liaise closely with the Special Needs Department and will meet on a regular basis.

13 The Support Worker will discuss with the Special Needs Manager any training needs and attend relevant courses.

14 The Support Worker will act at all times on behalf of the Association and may call upon the support of relevant departments at any time.

....
....

Example 4

Job Description of a Housing Association Housing Support Worker for People with Mental Health Problems and Learning Difficulties in Dispersed Tenancies

1 Tenant Support

– Offering appropriate personal support

– Assisting tenants in claiming benefits, personal budgeting and savings

– Maintaining personal and medical checks on all tenants, especially those regarded as being 'at risk', including contact with general practitioners, community psychiatric nurses, hospitals etc

– Checking that each house is kept in reasonable condition and cleanliness, and working with tenants to ensure they understand their responsibilities in this area and have the skills and resources necessary to carry them out

- Inducting new tenants into the association's facilities, assessing their support needs and helping them to deal with the practicalities of the move

- Helping tenants maintain a reasonable standard of personal hygiene and nutrition

- Liaising and working in conjunction with other workers including those responsible for the recruitment, work placement, work supervision and training of tenants

- Carrying out other tasks necessary to ensure the safety and well being of the tenants and to maximise their opportunities to manage their own lives

- Participating in a rota to provide cover for the out of hours telephone service for tenants, and dealing with emergencies and problems that arise

2 Housing Management

- Collecting rent and dealing with arrears

- Arranging for new tenants to move in, and for transfers of existing tenants.

- Carrying out all administrative and financial tasks associated with the management of the housing including keeping written records, correspondence, and accounting for money received and paid out

- Ordering repairs to houses and, in conjunction with the Association's Property Worker, ensuring that houses are properly finished and equipped

Example 5

Identified Support Tasks for Someone with Mental Health Problems

This list arises from our research on housing management in a wide range of local authorities and housing associations.

- Encourage to live with dignity and privacy, providing encouragement, care and assistance as required

- Maintain tenant's confidence

- Respect confidential information and records

- Explain tenancy agreements and ensure housing rights and obligations are understood

- Provide support to help tenants to sustain the tenancy, such as advice on dealing with rent arrears, and refer to relevant agencies where appropriate

- Identify support and care needs and refer to external bodies where appropriate eg social services, community nursing etc

- Identify when practical knowledge and skills are required to assist in maintaining independent housing and arrange training

- Assist when required with regard to personal care, hygiene, nutrition, domestic skills

- Offer individual advice in personal welfare

- Assist with requests concerning moves to different accommodation etc.

- Provide information on local community facilities

- Encourage to take advantage of community facilities, accompanying where necessary

- Assist in search for employment and training, including liaising with training agencies and potential employers

- Offer a befriending service

- Investigate and take action on complaints including disputes with neighbours

- Encourage and foster consideration for and by others

- Maintain personal and medical checks, especially on those regarded as 'at risk' including contact with GP, community nurse, hospital etc

- Assist in supervision of self–medication

- Take necessary action to get medical attention

- Notify next of kin etc in emergency

- Arrange systems for emergency contacts

- Arrange appropriate assistance at times of personal crisis

- Arrange help in areas such as decoration, replacement of furniture, draught proofing etc.

- Ensure common parts, gardens, paths, dustbins, dustbin areas are maintained and kept clean and tidy, and that means of escape are free from obstruction.

Chapter 2
Preparing for CCT

The ADC/IoH guide *Competition and Local Authority Housing Services* provides information on the strategic decisions which need to be addressed in preparation for CCT, and the legal framework within which these decisions have to be taken.

There are three key activities which need to be undertaken before moving to considerations about the writing of the contract documentation. These are:

• reviewing the objectives and policies of the service

• making strategic decisions over issues such as

   – the activities to be contracted out
   – the division of responsibilities between client and contractor
   – contract packaging
   – criteria for choosing the contractor
   – assessing performance
   – contract variation

• deciding on and starting to implement policies on tenant consultation

The aim of this chapter is to examine these three areas with particular attention to the implications for community care.

Service Review

*'The tendency is to become more aware of the gaps and want
something better when you start describing it.'*
Peter Kegg, quoted by Morris 1994:9

There can be no doubt that the exercise of preparation for CCT will
engage housing authorities in a close examination of their existing
practices and procedures. Walsh (1993) argues that one of the benefits
of the use of contracts in service provision is to clarify the nature of the
services that are provided, and the way in which they are provided.
Roles and responsibilities become more precisely defined and there is
closer control of both staff and costs. More bluntly CCT tells customers
exactly what they can expect for their money.

*'In determining what is either feasible or desirable with respect to
contracting out one therefore needs to know about the attributes of
the product and the way that it is produced; about the relationships
between the different actors and about the ethos in which those
actors expect to operate.'*
DoE 1992 para 2.10

The starting point for CCT is to establish a comprehensive review of the
existing housing service and to identify the principles which will lead to
the formation of the contract details. Issues to be addressed in
consultation with tenants, officers and members include:

- what services are provided?
- what services do tenants want?
- what are the service objectives?
- what are the strengths and weaknesses of the current service?
- what changes could improve the situation?
- how much does the service currently cost?
- how much are tenants prepared to pay – would they pay for an
  improved service?
- an analysis of staff functions
- a skills audit

An option which some authorities are pursuing is the formulation of the
results of this exercise into a Business or Service Plan, covering a three
to five year span, and addressing strategic objectives, priorities and
methods of service delivery. In Scotland there is a requirement for

authorities to produce a Housing Management Plan (HMP) detailing the housing management strategy. These must be prepared on a four yearly cycle, starting in 1994, with the exception of Glasgow which will do so every two years. HMPs should include policies on housing management, arrangements for tenant participation and preliminary structures and plans in regard to CCT.

The service plan or HMP should address the issues discussed in Chapter 1 relating to the nature of the housing management service and appropriate organisational arrangements.

Strategic Decisions

i)   *The Activities to be Contracted Out*

During the consultation process there have been significant revisions to the determination of which housing management functions are to be subject to compulsory competitive tendering.

The latest draft regulations at the time of writing, issued on 13 May 1994, could be summarised as covering:

- rent and service charge collection
- letting (but not the allocation) of property
- vacant properties
- tenancy management
- monitoring of repairs and maintenance contracts
- monitoring of caretaking and cleaning contracts

Each of these headings can be further broken down into the tasks which constitute each defined activity (but for exact terminology refer to the actual regulations.)

Rent and Service Charge Collection
- notifying rent and service charges to tenants and leaseholders

- monitoring rent and service charges paid by current and former tenants, and leaseholders

- collecting rents, service charges and contributions to tenant insurance schemes

- ensuring payment of rents and service charges (excluding service charge loans) including the arrears of current and former tenants, and leaseholders

- negotiating, monitoring and ensuring compliance with payment agreements for rent and service charge arrears

- recovering rent and service charge arrears

Letting of Property
- contacting nominated applicants for dwellings, offering allocated properties and arranging tenancy agreements

- processing applications for transfers and exchanges, including management transfers, interviewing tenants and making recommendations in connection with such applications

- accompanying applicants on viewing visits and undertaking home visits to tenants

- processing applications and letting garages, parking spaces and stores relating to qualifying properties

Tenancies
- issuing tenancy agreements and leases

- ensuring compliance with agreements and leases, taking action to stop or prevent breaches of agreements and issuing warnings

- taking action to control disturbances, harassment and domestic disputes involving tenants, including attendance at scene where required, liaising with tenants, residents and specialist agencies to deal with conflicts or make recommendations

Vacant Properties
- arranging the vacating of properties and taking possession

- inspecting vacant properties and arranging clearance, repairs, cleaning, decoration, security and maintenance

- preventing vandalism and illegal occupation

- obtaining possession of properties occupied by illegal occupants

Repairs and Maintenance

- receiving requests for responsive repairs, assessing and transmitting requests to contractors

- monitoring and ensuring progress with responsive repairs

- monitoring performance of contractors, carrying out post repair inspections and reporting compliance by contractors

- reporting contractor performance

- carrying out inspections to ascertain condition and whether a house is occupied

- receiving and assessing claims under right to repair and right to compensation for improvement schemes and recommending action, including arranging the payment of compensation

Caretaking and Cleaning

- operating concierge services

- assessing condition of common areas and grounds of multi–occupant dwelling blocks

- ordering repairs, maintenance, cleaning, rubbish removal and disinfestation services of common areas in multi–occupancy buildings

- reporting contractor performance

These defined activities are those which must be contracted out, and as such represent a minimum. Authorities can contract out tasks not specified if they wish to do so. There are also certain tasks which could be seen to be a joint responsibility of both contractor and client side, and provision may need to be made for these:

- dealing with enquiries
- providing information to tenants

- advice services
- dealing with complaints
- liaising with tenants

Decisions have to be made both about the scope of the activities which will be constituted as housing management as discussed in Chapter 1 and also about which of these activities are to be contracted out. It must be borne in mind that only 95 per cent of each defined activity has to be included in the contract, and that where less than 25% of an employee's job is spent on defined activities it can be exempt from CCT. This allows scope for those authorities who wish it, to keep certain community care functions on the client side. A decision on this will relate to whether it has been agreed to provide a specialist service for community care tenants or to include it as part of a generic service.

ii)   *The Division of Responsibilities between Client and Contractor*

There is no legal requirement to split the organisation between client and contractor divisions except during the actual competition process. However, most authorities are instigating at least some formal division of responsibilities, which may involve considerable organisational change. This division is referred to as the client/contractor split.

The DoE have made it clear that there is no fixed model which will determine the precise nature of the relationship between client and contractor. This will allow each authority to have regard to its local situation, and to adopt a structure which is responsive to that situation. The authority is expected to retain its role in setting policy and strategy, and in ensuring that such policies and strategies are effectively attained.

The area in which the respective roles of client and contractor are clear is in relation to the structure, rather than the content, of the contract. Authorities will have to decide on the most effective structures for achieving the client/contractor split within their organisation. An analysis of existing roles will reveal what proportion of a person's time is currently spent on activities which are to be retained on the client side, and what proportion will need to be consigned to the contractor side. Authorities may take the opportunity for radical reorganisation of existing working practices, others will prefer to adopt a more minimal response. Either way, the choice lies between a 'hard' split or a 'soft' split. A hard split implies a complete separation of the client and contractor role, whilst a soft split indicates that an individual post can have responsibilities on both the client and the contractor side. (The case studies of pilot authorities in Chapter 5 offer contrasting examples in this respect.)

Authorities need to address how functions relating to community care will be performed under CCT. Many authorities already have a post covering the strategic and enabling role of housing in community care, others subsume it within non–specialist posts. Either way someone on the client side needs to retain a responsibility in relation to joint planning with health and social service authorities, and for liaison with voluntary and other agencies.

The extent to which such a post becomes extended into housing management activities has also to be addressed. This needs to take account of the extent to which the authority is restricting the contract to the defined activities, or taking a comprehensive approach. If for example, allocations (not a defined activity) is to be included in the contract, a decision has to be made as to whether the contractor is also to allocate to community care users and/or other community care groups or whether the interests of such tenants would best be served by retaining this function on the client side. There are a number of reasons why the latter course might be advantageous:

- the contractor has to accept the tenant provided a suitable property can be found

- the authority can take a district wide perspective and allocate to a location which best suits the needs of the tenant – particularly if areas are operating on contracts with different levels of service

- the authority can utilise existing relationships with support services

- the authority may be in a better position to balance the relative merits of different types of accommodation – sheltered, supported, independent.

The exempt proportion relating to the 5 per cent flexibility in the competition requirement noted above allows some scope to retain on the client side some aspects of the defined activities relating to community care. Another possibility is to use the exemption relating to the retention of posts on the client side where such posts involve less than 25 per cent of their time in defined activities. Residential workers are exempt in any case, but other posts which have an element of specialism could be retained on the client side. These include:

- mobile wardens
- tenancy support workers
- welfare workers
- special needs officers
- youth case workers
- housing case workers
- support workers
- tenant liaison officers

iii) *Packaging*

The government consultation paper, *Competing for Quality in Housing* (1992) suggests that moves to a comprehensive housing service are not threatened by the division of the service between different agents. Authorities may or may not agree with this view, but they need to consider the nature of the organisations from which these agents might come, and the sort of service they are prepared to offer. The main candidates other than in–house teams are housing associations and the private sector. These will have different views on the nature of the service they are willing to tender for, and this is particularly true in relation to community care aspects.

> *'Housing associations in particular felt able to provide the whole range of service. Private sector agencies felt, however, that they would not wish to be involved in policy–making, nor would they wish to provide for special needs, although there was evidence that they might if the price was right.'*
> DoE 1992 para 6.4

Authorities may consider that certain specialist areas of housing management could be let separately; one obvious candidate for this is sheltered housing. Other forms of supported accommodation could also be in a separate package. Again, the whole of such a specialist service could be offered, or it could be further sub–divided with the property side either being let separately from the care side, or under a different type of agreement with the same contractor as in Case Study 2, Chapter 5.

In the same way it would be possible to contract out a basic housing management service to one agency (for example a private contractor) and to contract separately for a more specialised community care service with another (for example a specialist housing association). This approach may be necessary if no contractor has all the skills which would be required for a generic service. It is, therefore, important for authorities to give considerable thought to which local or national agencies might be expected to have an interest in tendering and for what type of package. In particular authorities should consider approaching smaller specialist housing organisations, and voluntary organisations, who might not themselves have thought of tendering, but who could provide an effective service. The authority should where necessary, assist and support them in the tendering process. The aim should be to achieve a partnership between client and contractor based on mutual trust and goodwill.

The other consideration in regard to packaging relates to how the different parts of an authority's stock are divided between contracts. Different areas of an authority's stock have different characteristics, and are likely to be more or less attractive to contractors. Problems may arise for generally deprived inner city areas or peripheral estates, for scattered rural communities, and for areas where there are high numbers of vulnerable tenants, perhaps because they are located near a psychiatric hospital or because there is a high proportion of older people.

The involvement of tenants in the specification process, and their definition of the service they would prefer, raises the issue that where separate contracts are let for different areas within one authority, the level of service could vary considerably. This has implications for rent setting. It is possible to have a core rent for an optimum service, with increases or reductions for those who want more or less. This would however have to operate across a whole area, and not to individual tenants. For example, tenants in one area might ask for a superior caretaking service, or a door to door rent collection. Similarly, in an area with a high incidence of people with mental health problems, there might be a perception that a more supportive service was needed, covering all tenants, and fostering a sense of an integrated and caring community. Obviously, there are housing benefit implications here, and the District Auditor would need to accept the position.

iv)   Criteria for Choosing the Contractor

The procedures that will be used to select the contractor need to be addressed early in the process of preparation for CCT. The procedures decided upon will have an important bearing on the contract documentation. The strategies adopted in assessing both invitations to tender, and evaluation of bids, must be precise enough to compare the relative merits of different approaches to, and methods of, service delivery.

At the pre–tender stage the authority will receive expressions of interest, both in response to advertisement and through direct approaches. These will provide the basis from which to select contractors to include in a list of those who will be invited to tender. Authorities can use questionnaires to assess availability for inclusion, although EC regulations mean that the information requested should be restricted to those which assess economic and financial standing, ability, and technical capacity.

It is at this stage that authorities with a concern for the social, welfare and community care aspects of housing management, can establish the likely responsiveness of potential contractors to fulfil obligations and requirements in this field. Information which can be sought at the pre–tender stage which might assist in assessing the ability of a potential contractor to be sensitive to community care needs include:

•   assessment of education and professional qualifications
•   availability of expertise, including any special competences and experience
•   ability to cope with the profile of the work, or unplanned, or urgent work
•   references which demonstrate relevant experience
•   information on past contracts
•   access to library and research facilities, training and supervision
(Adapted from LGMB 1994 para 33)

When it comes to the question of the evaluation of tenders the authority should bear in mind that EU Regulations permit two alternative ways of assessing bids:

- the most economically advantageous
- the lowest price

The former allows consideration of criteria other than price, notably quality and cost effectiveness, to be taken into account when awarding contracts. Local authorities are free to determine the criteria they wish to use, provided they are relevant, have a commercial orientation, are non–discriminatory and are not anti–competitive. Authorities can balance the relative merits of price and quality but must publicise the way in which they intend to determine this.

The LGMB Guidance (1994) suggests that it is important to explore the following aspects:

- the qualification and experience of the individual professional staff providing the services
- availability and ability to cope with unplanned aspects of the contract
- location of offices and proximity of staff
- level of resources that a contractor intends to devote to the contract
- arrangements for maintaining the required level of expertise and knowledge
- access and availability in emergencies and out of hours
- proposed race relations and equal opportunities policies
- proposed methods of communication between contractor and client and/or users.

Many of the points here have a particular relevance to tenants with community care needs. Tenderers must be asked for sufficient information and documentation, where necessary, in relation to community care issues. Authorities, therefore, need to consider whether they feel that the writing of output based specifications will result in insufficient detail upon which to question potential contractors. This is especially the case where generic, as opposed to specialist, services are to be let. Contractors will need to be asked to demonstrate that they will take account of individual needs and difficulties. Unless informed otherwise they will prefer to believe that they are expected to provide a standard service to a homogenous group of people.

v) **Assessing Performance**

*'Housing Management contracts will be difficult to monitor. It is
not as easy as measuring pool temperatures or the length of grass.'*
McIntosh 1993: 40

It is necessary to think at the outset about how the contractor's
performance is to be assessed since monitoring procedures and criteria
will need to be laid down in the contract conditions. Also, evaluation
should be borne in mind when the specification is being written. Any
performance indicators and targets to be used should be included in the
specification, and in the framing of each element of the specification
thought needs to be given as to how it will be assessed.

There has been considerable interest in the whole field of performance
assessment in the last few years coinciding with the spread of the
contracting of services. Particular emphasis has been placed on ideas of
Quality.

One approach has been for some organisations to adopt British
Standard 5750. This incorporates a series of standards relating to the
procedures and criteria that an organisation needs to follow in order to
obtain a certificate of quality assurance. BS 5750 has been awarded to a
number of housing and social care organisations (Walsh 1993) but there
is some controversy over its use in this context.

Whilst the possession of a BS 5750 certificate may indicate quality in
relation to the ability to perform general procedures to a satisfactory
standards, it is not a guarantee of quality of outcome in a specific area
of work.

*'The adoption of formalistic quality procedures, detailed in
contract specifications, is unlikely to produce quality services in
housing and social care. Approaches to certification that are more
responsive to the particular context involved might be developed,
for example, through social services or housing professionals
establishing their own certification bodies. Quality assurance,
properly developed, can reduce monitoring costs and improve
delivery standards, but much remains to be done to develop an
approach that fits housing and social care.*
Walsh 1993: 79

Recognition of the limitations of BS 5750 in relation to housing has prompted publication of the guide *Total Quality: An Introduction to Quality Management in Social Housing* (Catterick 1992). This attempts to improve and refine the model of BS 5750 and suggest a framework whereby housing organisations can achieve the best possible quality service.

More practical guidelines are available in the Institute's *Housing Management Standards Manual*, a source which seems inherently more useful to those concerned to establish methods to gauge performance standards.

The concept of Quality brings together ideas of quality control (monitoring performance after the event) and quality assurance (establishing procedures and systems before the work is undertaken in order to ensure that performance will be effectively achieved). Some combination of the two is necessary, but more investment in quality assurance may mean that quality control can be de–emphasised as fewer mistakes will be made. Therefore, in the contracting situation, consideration needs to be given not only to the monitoring undertaken by the client, but also to the monitoring and review undertaken by the contractors.

There are a number of general issues which the client has to ensure:

- a framework and a timetable should be set for the monitoring process

- default procedures need to be in place and understood

- appropriate community care expertise should be available on the client side for monitoring to take place

- monitoring procedures need to be integrated with liaison arrangements with health and social services agencies. This is essential in order for their views on appropriate monitoring to be incorporated, and so that they become aware of any problems in performance

Monitoring by the Contractor
The contract conditions should establish what is expected of the contractors in reviewing their own performance. It could be stipulated

that contractors should have or be applying for BS 5750. An alternative approach would be to stipulate a set of procedures more tailored to housing management by taking examples from the guidance mentioned above.

The issues identified here are relevant to the service provided to all tenants, but it is important that the needs of community care tenants are not neglected. Contractors could be expected to pay special attention to the following:

• instituting regular liaison meetings with representatives of tenants with community care needs as well as attention to community care issues in general dialogue with tenants

• maintaining regular liaison with health and social services agencies

• setting up procedures for dealing with any complaints by community care users

Feedback from these sources should be used by the contractor both to monitor performance on an ongoing basis, and to assess performance in relation to the specification.

Monitoring by the Client
The type of monitoring to be carried out will depend to a large extent on the nature of the specification. 'Tight' specifications which include detailed and prescriptive procedures, seem on the surface to make monitoring easy, when compared with 'loose' specifications which are expressed in more general terms. However, there are questions over the practicalities of monitoring procedures. This is a particularly important point in relation to community care because of the emphasis on personal service and the meeting of individual needs which are not easily measurable in the framework of a set of indicators. Housing management is as much about the way in which things are done as about what is done.

There may be some performance indicators which can be used to monitor performance and which can be written into specifications (examples are given in chapter 4). Monitoring by the client may then involve checking and interpreting these indicators. However, this is unlikely to be sufficient to ensure that a high quality service is being provided.

> '*Most of the views expressed about monitoring were the other side
> of the coin from points made about the specification, since the
> ability to monitor is dependent on the nature of the specification.
> The most difficult activities to monitor were therefore seen as being
> those where the contractor would have a direct personal
> relationship with the tenant. There was, however, a contrary point
> of view that if tenants were involved in the monitoring it was in fact
> very simple to monitor by exception, based on the degree of tenant
> complaint. This, in turn, produced a further view that the tenants
> least likely to complain, ie the elderly and the vulnerable were
> those who most needed services involving a personal relationship.*'
> DoE 1993 para 4.66

Example
It may be easy to monitor whether a contractor has gone through the
tenancy agreement at sign up. But, for an elderly person, has it been
checked whether he or she is hard of hearing, or confused, or suffering
from senile dementia. If any of those apply, what has been done about
it? Or if the person has some form of learning difficulty what steps have
been taken to ensure comprehension? Has it been suggested an
advocate or relative be present? Has the housing officer been patient,
willing to repeat key points and ask for feedback?

The monitoring of procedures is possible by ensuring the contractor
keeps adequate records which can be inspected. Information systems
should be regularly checked. Particular attention needs to be paid in
situations where the contractor may be held to be in default through the
failure of another agency to provide adequate support to a tenant, for
example where a care contract with social services stipulates that
benefits will be negotiated for the tenant, and failure to do so results in
rent arrears. But the personal aspects of the service can only be assessed
by direct surveillance or through feedback from the users. Surveillance
is used by social services inspectors in assessing residential
establishments, but is more difficult outside supported accommodation
schemes. Nevertheless, it would be possible for the client to, for
example, sit in on a number of interviews to assess the way they are
undertaken. However, the use of this form of monitoring is likely to be
restricted since it could be time–consuming and expensive. Spot checks

and the interviewing of participants after the event may be useful as additional ways of checking performance.

Monitoring through feedback from tenants is potentially very useful.

> '*Tenants, it is important to realise, can be immensely useful in monitoring contracts. The authority ought to make use of the thousands of eyes and ears it has available.*'
> McIntosh 1993: 40

> '*To know what the users of a service think and feel about such a service is clearly an important part of evaluation. It has been argued that consumer evaluation has to take precedence as accountability to clients has higher priority than accountability to agency or profession.*'
> Atkinson and Elliott 1994: 156

One of the problems of tenant involvement in monitoring is that tenants will not necessarily have the same priorities and interests as authorities. A further problem is that they are not directly party to the contract, although they are central to it. This means that effectively they have no power to opt out; they do not have real control. Since the issue of quality of service, in regard particularly to personal service elements, is one that can best be judged by the users of that service it becomes essential to find ways for tenants to have a real voice in the monitoring process.

> '*Where tenants wish to become more directly involved in the contract monitoring process it will be for the authority to agree with them the arrangements which need to be put in place. These can include simple complaints procedures, customer satisfaction surveys, monitoring panels and, ultimately, giving tenant groups management control. Whatever model is chosen it will be important that the authority, contractor and tenants fully understand the service standards required by the contract, the role of each party and the relationship, the arrangements for reporting and initiating action and the lines of accountability and responsibility for the contract.*
> DoE 1994 para 30

The more powerless and vulnerable tenants are, the more need they have of the personal relationship, and yet the less confidence and

opportunity they are likely to have in articulating their views.
Authorities need therefore to recognise that the areas of housing
management that relate to community care are going to be those where
it is least easy to elicit options. Mechanisms need to be adopted to
overcome this, and will broadly be the same as discussed in the
following section on tenant consultation.

vi)   *Contract Variation*

One of the problems in relation to the writing of the contract will be
that it is impossible to specify for every eventuality. Authorities must,
therefore, decide how they will address the issue of variation in the
contract, particularly as the contractor may be entitled to charge for
additional work incurred through unspecified activities. Authorities
writing 'tight' specifications (as in Case Study 2 Chapter 5) may feel that
they can predict and allow for any contingency. In practice this is
unlikely to be the case. Other authorities (as in Case Study 1) are
writing into the specifications that the client has the right to vary the
contract in certain regards. Too much scope for variation however may
frighten off potential contractors who will be wary of putting in bids for
work which is not precisely detailed. Contract variation is perhaps
particularly likely to occur when dealing with tenants with community
care needs who may often require more individualised treatment than
others.

It is probable that some of the problems in this regard will only be
apparent once the contract is running. Monitoring will, therefore, be at
its most crucial during the course of that first contract, and detailed
information should be collated and processed to be considered at the
review stage towards the end of the contract.

Some authorities (as Case Study 1) have seen the advantage of a
'dummy run' wherein the service is run under contract conditions. A
review of this dummy run will serve to highlight problem areas which
could then be more precisely addressed in the contract documentation
before the contract is let for real.

Running the service under contract conditions may be particularly
helpful to community care groups who may have difficulty in
conceptualising a service in the abstract, and in assessing how the

contract will affect them. It will also give agencies who work with tenants in a support and/or caring role to evaluate the impact of the changes on their own services.

Tenant Consultation

The Housing Act 1985, as amended by the 1993 Leasehold Reform, Housing and Urban Development Act, requires authorities in England and Wales to consult tenants and consider their representations in regard to:

- the terms of the agreement, including the standards of service to be required
- the selection and identity of the contractor
- the performance of the contractor including enforcement action

The major change introduced by the 1993 Act is that tenants will not have the same right of veto that they have with other forms of management transfer.

> '*No; tenants will not be able to impose a veto on the successful candidate after the [CCT] process has been gone through, but they will have rights to consultation on the terms of an agreement, including those resulting from CCT and they will be involved in monitoring the contract.*'
> Sir George Young, Commons debate, reported in *Inside Housing* 1993: 6

The DoE published more detailed guidance in March 1994, *Tenant Involvement in Housing Management*, in which it makes clear that authorities are expected to do more than satisfy the legal minimum, and to adopt practices which take into account local circumstances.

The Guidance suggests a number of general principles.

> '*Information provided for individual tenants may be different from that provided to tenant organisations and their representatives. Where tenant organisations and representatives are involved in formal discussions with an authority it will be important that they have access to full versions of key documents, such as contract*

specifications. Where tenants are being consulted on a general basis, authorities should provide summaries which address the issues of most interest to tenants or which have the most impact on the services to be provided. Authorities should also consider whether special arrangements might be required where tenants have special needs.

Individual tenants and their collective organisations should have access to sufficient quality and quantity of information to enable them to play a constructive part in and make informed judgements about the content and operation of contracts and contractors. The DoE suggests that information about resources and costs will be as important as that concerning standards of service and content of contracts.'
ADC/IoH 1994: 8/10

The issues in which tenants should be involved include:

* establishing selection criteria
* the interviewing of contractors and selection process
* compiling the shortlist
* evaluating tenders

In Scotland there is no legislative framework in regard to tenant consultation; any arrangements are voluntary. However, there is a stated commitment to the involvement of tenants in the level, type and quality of service, and in the selection process. As in England and Wales, it is the authority which will have the statutory responsibility for the choice of contractor.

More detailed information on tenant involvement is available in Module 8 'Tenant Involvement' of the ADC/IoH Manual.

Tenants with community care needs have as much right to participate in the consultation process as any other, and the process of doing so should allow a valuable opportunity for them to suggest improvements in the way the service is currently delivered, in particular their expectations as to what the role of housing departments should, or could, be in assisting the process of independent living. In this respect tenants should be involved in planning and inter–agency liaison as discussed in Chapter 1 where they can feed into the setting of objectives and the nature of provision. More specifically in regard to CCT their input is particularly important at the contract specification stage since existing routinised housing management procedures may lack the personal dimension that is necessary for individual cases.

> *'Even when a user's own articulation of need is heard it is often ignored because it does not fit established service provision.'*
> Arnold et al 1993:24

> *'The use of the term "consumer" itself brings with it the suggestion of choice in a market place filled with a variety of services... That the client in community care is not in this position does not mean that their input is not valuable, but it can mean that it has limited perspective if not all options are known and understood. Clients may well have valuable information about services which are lacking and which they think they would find helpful, but there may be options which no one knows they want until they have been presented with the idea.'*
> Atkinson and Elliott 1994:157

It is also important that tenderers are requested to make presentations to tenants, to answer their questions and to submit documentation for their inspection. Contractors should be aware of the sort of service that tenants, including those with community care needs, expect so that their views and requirements are not forgotten once the contract is let.

Clearly there are a number of problems in bringing community care on to the agenda of tenants:

- how to persuade general needs tenants that community care should be an important issue
- how to resolve issues about differential levels of service which all tenants have to pay for
- how to overcome resistance to having 'problem' people as neighbours
- how to find and make contact with tenants with community care needs
- how to encourage and enable tenants with community care needs to participate and articulate their needs on an equal footing

Every effort should be made to involve tenants with community care needs in a meaningful dialogue rather than merely to inform them of processes. This may require skills which housing staff do not normally possess, in which case they should be given appropriate training. The assistance of specialist workers or organisations which serve particular community care groups may be useful. A major problem will be trying to fit what may be a time–consuming process into the necessary time–scale, especially if tenant consultation in general is not well–developed in an authority.

Methods of achieving involvement could include:

- the identification of individuals from existing records, and contacting them individually
- advertising for feedback in the local press and on local radio
- speaking at day centres, support groups, carers' groups etc
- contacting hospitals about their discharge programmes and arranging to speak to patients involved in them
- visiting sheltered housing and supported accommodation schemes
- visiting temporary accommodation
- conducting small group discussions for targeted groups
- seeking the opinion of advocates, and local and national agencies
- providing practical help such as accessible venues, transport, signers, hearing loops, documents in large print, braille and on audio–tape

'Developing effective participation, particularly with individuals and groups who have had little or no previous involvement, is likely to be a gradual process requiring a variety of approaches and methods, involving experimentation and learning by all concerned. The effectiveness of these processes will therefore need to be regularly and jointly reviewed. Authorities will need to build up relationships and credibility with voluntary organisations, users and carers, many of whom may have had experience of consultation which is tokenistic and does not lead to change.'
Community Care Plans (NCVO 1990) quoted in Walsh 1993:80

Checklist: Preparing for CCT

☑ Have you carried out a review of the existing service?

☑ Within this have you addressed all the issues relating to the social and welfare role of housing management and the options for meeting community care needs?

☑ Have these been incorporated into a service policy statement, a business plan or a housing management plan?

☑ Have you decided whether to contract out only the defined activities or a comprehensive service?

☑ Have you considered the community care implications of this decision?

☑ Have you examined the tasks involved within each of the defined activities to assess what, if any, different or additional arrangements are needed for those tenants with community care needs?

☑ Have you decided on the nature of the client/contractor split?

☑ Within this, have you addressed how to apportion community care responsibilities?

☑ Have you examined the potential for using the exempt proportion for community care activities?

☑ Have you decided on the most appropriate way to approach packaging for instance with specialist services such as supported accommodation or sheltered housing contracted out separately from general housing, and if so, will the care element be offered separately?

☑ Have you considered the possibilities and implications of differential levels of service in different areas, perhaps where there are high numbers of vulnerable tenants?

☑ Have you decided on strategies and criteria for choosing the contractor?

☑ Have you addressed how performance will be monitored?

☑ Have you envisaged what problems might occur in relation to variation of the contract and how these might be overcome?

☑ Have you considered the value of a dummy run?

☑ Have you made adequate arrangements for tenant consultation, especially in relation tenants with community care needs?

Chapter 3
Contract Documentation

The aim of this chapter is to cover what needs to be included in the contract documentation. The most important element of this is the specification and this is considered separately in the following chapter. Nevertheless, thought also needs to be given to other elements of the contract which could exert considerable influence on the achievement of community care objectives. The aspects considered here are:

- contract conditions
- liaison with other agencies
- training for community care
- assessment and care plans
- contracts for support and care

A review of the existing service suggested in the previous chapter will be invaluable in the process of drawing up the contract. Clarification of the aims and objectives of the service is essential if the contract documentation is to be internally consistent.

Contract Conditions

The contract conditions contain the express terms relating to the general performance of the contract and set out the rights and obligations of both parties. Included are such matters as:

- definition of terms
- method of payment

- procedures in regard to variations and unforeseen circumstances
- default and damage conditions
- provision for determining the contract
- quality assurance
- tendering instructions
- pricing systems
- settlement of disputes
- liability and indemnity

The specifications describe in detail the work to be carried out and the expected standards and quality to be achieved.

There are also certain general issues which could be included within the documentation in the contract conditions, or as an introduction to the specifications, or in relevant places within the text. Such matters relate to relevant legislation, the housing stock, council policies, tenant relations, information exchange, staffing levels etc. Other information which should be included consists of:

- customer care
  - staffing
  - office/reception
  - telephone communication
  - face to face communication
  - correspondence
  - home visits
- information and advice
- equal opportunities
- liaison with other agencies
- liaison with other LA departments
- record keeping and confidentiality
- relationships with other contractors
- training
- relations with tenants
- monitoring

A further breakdown of these matters is available in the CCT publications by the AMA (1994) and the ADC/IoH (1993/94), upon which this list has been based. Both of these publications make passing, but limited, reference to special needs and community care issues. It would appear something more detailed is required. This could include a statement of the authority's principles on community care services to vulnerable tenants, and policies on supported accommodation and independent living. All the aspects mentioned above should be spelt out in more detail with tenants with community care needs in mind. For example, conditions on customer care could include the following:

The Office
- disabled access – ramps, lightweight doors, low handles etc
- disabled parking
- bells, leaflets etc within reach of wheelchair
- disabled toilets
- adequate seating
- panic buttons for staff
- visual and auditory call system, where installed
- posters and leaflets on carers' groups, support groups, voluntary organisations etc
- confidential interview areas

Communication
- information available in braille, large print, and audio tape
- interpreter for speech and hearing impaired
- acceptance of limitations on communication eg
    - reading/writing
    - remembering
    - formulating questions
    - understanding concepts
    - sitting still
    - concentrating
    - articulating
    - thinking about change
    - relating to others
    - eye contact
- people should be treated as individuals, not as stereotypical members of a category
- higher levels then normal of anxiety and stress should be anticipated
- it may be difficult to overcome unrealistic expectations
- bizarre, unconventional or disconcerting behaviour may be displayed
- reasonable attempts should be made to cope with difficult behaviour, before seeking assistance, but not at the expense of personal safety

Readers are also referred to Chapter 12 'Housing Services for People with Special Needs' of the Institute's *Housing Management Standards Manual*, which presents a detailed list of standards for making services responsive to tenants who are in any way vulnerable.

Liaison With Other Agencies

Formal processes, as discussed in Chapter 1, should have been established with other agencies involved in community care. Such processes should be described, perhaps with supporting documentation such as the social services community care plan and joint planning strategy statements. All agencies with which the contractor might have to liaise over community care issues should be listed, with a named contact person wherever possible eg

- social services
- educational services
- community and leisure services
- housing benefit
- refuse collection
- environmental health
- community health services
- hospitals
- residential homes
- other housing providers
- relevant voluntary organisations
- DSS
- probation
- solicitors
- police
- tenant groups

Training for Community Care

Requirements can be built into the contract which specify the skills the contractor is expected to have and/or to acquire. In all cases, but particularly where a generalist service is to be contracted out, the interests of vulnerable tenants need to be protected by ensuring that the contractor's staff are aware of the issues involved. Training should seek not only to develop individual skills, but awareness of the work of other agencies involved in care, perhaps by joint training and 'skills exchange' sessions. Other issues which should be addressed include:

- the role of the housing service in community care
- relevant legislation
- needs of different community care groups
- equal opportunities and non discrimination
- interviewing skills
- the assessment process
- aids, adaptation and improvements
- health and safety
- user rights

Particular attention should be paid to training in regard to people with mental health problems. Housing officers frequently cite their lack of knowledge and experience in this field, and it is recommended that the contractor is obliged to ensure that all staff are trained in the legislation, symptomatology and procedures for dealing with mental health problems.

Assessment and Care Plans

In the preparation for CCT the opportunity should have been taken for the housing authority to review its part in the assessment process and to negotiate agreements with other agencies and involved parties as described in Chapter 1. Such arrangements should then be spelt out in the contract documentation, along with the expectations and requirements of the contractor. These would include:

- being aware of the council's community care policy
- liaison with those involved in care – statutory and voluntary agencies, informal carer, relatives, friends, neighbours
- participation in all community care assessments in which local authority housing was, or might be involved
- participation in care plan reviews
- alerting the relevant agencies if it was felt an assessment might be appropriate

- liaison with the tenant over the progress of a request for community care services
- participating in case conferences
- being available to care managers/key workers
- knowing how to contact care managers/key workers
- bringing to the attention of care managers when care plans appear not to be working

The contractor would need to be made aware of the current and potential extent of the frequency with which any of the above might occur, the length of time that might be involved, and the names of individual contacts of those who might be involved in a care plan. It is particularly important to allow for variation in the contract in this area.

The contract documentation should detail the range of individuals with whom the contractor might have to work.

Example of those who might be involved in the assessment and care plan of someone with learning difficulties or mental health problems.

Health Authority	Social Services	Housing LA/HA
Hospital Manager	Officer in Charge	Housing Manager
Nursing Officer	*Care Manager*	*Special Needs Officer*
CPN	Social Worker	Housing Officer
Psychiatrist	OT	*Warden*
Psychologist	Key Worker	Tenancy Support Worker
Physiotherapist	*Group Worker*	*Caretaker/Concierge*
	'Homemaker'	

Contracts for Support and Care

'Local housing officers say their role is not geared to support and they are not competent to make arrangements, nor do they have time. In ordinary housing a housing officer should aim to ensure the tenancy does not fail – they should not just allocate the property and then leave the tenant to cope. One possibility would be a proper contract, setting out all the support/care arrangements, with the housing officer monitoring and imposing some sort of

sanction if arrangements break down.'
Project Leader

An examination of the potential for the social role of housing
management within community care as discussed in Chapter 1 will have
informed the authority's decision about the nature of the support role,
both in supported accommodation projects and in mainstream housing,
and by whom this role will be carried out. If an authority retains on the
client side posts such as tenancy support worker or resettlement officer
it will have to make clear in the contract documentation precisely what
the scope of such a post is, and where the boundary is between the
contractor's and client's responsibility.

Guidance for this could be taken from existing support agreements with
social service departments (service level agreements) or housing
associations (management agreements). The contractor would also
need to be informed of the criteria which would trigger the need for
such a support worker, and any cost implications.

An example from a management agreement between a housing
association and a health authority is provided (Example 1 at the end of
the chapter) which clearly defines the distribution of responsibilities.
Other examples can be found in the Institute's *Housing Management
Standards Manual.*

One possibility is that housing officer involvement in community care
plans could be formalised in the nature of a three way contract between
social services in the person of the care manager/key worker, the
housing service in the person of the housing officer, and the community
care user, with the expectations and responsibilities of each party laid
out. The pilot authority in Case Study 2 (Chapter 5) plans a similar
approach. For instance on the housing side the tenants could agree to
learn to maintain the property in good order and co–exist peacefully
with neighbours, whilst the housing officer might agree to visit on a
regular basis, to make sure the garden was tended, to liaise with
neighbours and to attend review meetings. The potential for this can be
built into the contract documentation, and although it might have the
appearance of a contract within a contract, it would allow for the
individual problems of tenants to be addressed, rather then relying on
generalisations contained within the specification. Models already exist
in some special needs housing associations, and voluntary agencies in
the field, in the form of Individual Care Plans, or Individual Programme

Plans. An example of a support plan is provided at the end of the chapter as Example 2.

By extension this could apply also to tenants not under a care plan, but who, nonetheless, have community care needs. In a case where no other support worker was available the housing officer might be called upon to perform functions in the social and welfare field, which could be seen as necessary in the sustaining of the tenancy, as outlined in Chapter 1. This could be defined minimally, for example personal visits to check that the tenant is managing in an unspecified way, or more comprehensively, covering all the aspects of the social role listed in Chapter 1, such as establishing that benefits are being received, the property cared for, the tenant has occupation and is in contact with neighbours, that hospital appointments are being kept, medication taken etc. A comprehensive example from an agency providing support to single homeless people is included as Example 3 at the end of the chapter in which it will be noted that support needs are divided into high, medium and low.

Although the possibilities and implications of such support arrangements are far–reaching, especially in cost terms, it is important for each authority to consider the extent to which it wishes to address the social and welfare needs of its tenants in the contract, particularly the most vulnerable. If this is not done at the present moment the opportunity may be lost, as the scope for change at a later date will be limited.

Checklist: Contract Documentation

☑ Have you decided how to include community care considerations in the general conditions of the contract?

☑ Have you identified those agencies with which a contractor might be expected to liaise in the course of working with tenants with community care needs?

☑ Have you clearly identified processes and procedures for liaison with such agencies?

☑ Have you considered what skills you expect the contractor to have which will affect the ability to work with community care groups, and what additional training should be required?

☑ Have you addressed to what extent the contractor is to be involved in assessment and care plans and laid out the relevant procedures and contact persons?

☑ Have you looked at the potential for contracts in regard to support and care?

....

Example 1

A Management And Support Agreement Between A Housing Association And A Health Authority

This housing association, originally founded to house single people, has in recent years become more involved in supported accommodation. It has a number of partnerships and agreements with other statutory and voluntary organisations. This example relates to supportive accommodation for people with mental health problems. The Schedules referred to are not reproduced here.

a) The housing association will be responsible for:

i)   ensuring that the selection of tenants by the Health Authority is in accordance with the association's referral/selection assessment procedure;

ii)   lettings, including preparing and signing tenancy agreements and discussing their contents with tenants or their advocates;

iii)   administering tenancy agreements ie carrying out its obligations as landlord and making sure that tenants carry out theirs. See separate schedule on Assured Tenancy Agreements; (Schedule 8).

iv)   setting and collecting rents from tenants and taking action on arrears;

v)   advising tenants on housing related welfare benefits in close liaison with Health Authority care staff;

vi)   undertaking legal action to evict tenants where necessary as set out in Schedule 3;

vii)   maintaining and decorating the property on a cycle as set out in Schedule 4;

viii)   ensuring that the house meets all relevant statutory requirements, including training tenants and staff in fire drill procedures and record keeping;

ix) carrying out the financial responsibilities as set out in Schedule 5 and in particular keeping accounts for the property covering housing management, maintenance and landlord's services;

x) repairing and replacing all furniture and equipment other than that belonging to tenants and taking an annual inventory of furniture;

xi) undertaking physical adaptations to the building to meet tenants' needs provided that funds are available;

xii) assisting in the identification of alternative accommodation in accordance with its move on policy as set out in Schedule 6 for tenants who would prefer and benefit from more independent housing;

xiii) insuring the building, fixtures, fittings and contents other than the personal possessions of tenants and staff;

xiv) employing staff to carry out these tasks (Schedule 7);

xv) at least weekly visits by management staff;

xvi) participating in the community integration of tenants;

xvii) participating in a Steering Group and other liaison meetings as agreed for the management of the house

These duties should be seen as complementary to those of the Health Authority.

b) The Health Authority will be responsible for:

i) selecting tenants for specific flats according to agreed criteria (Schedule 2);

ii) advising the Housing Association on the allocation of flats within the property. This will be done by the Health Authority support workers attached to a house;

iii) ensuring tenants' support needs are met including implementing individual care plans, providing personal care where agreed, ensuring health care is provided as necessary;

iv) enabling tenants to develop social, educational and daily living skills and to participate in community activities to their maximum potential;

v) undertaking and enabling tenants to be involved in housekeeping tasks including cleaning, cooking, laundry, purchase of food and household goods and gardening as appropriate;

vi) advising tenants on welfare benefits in close liaison with Housing Association staff;

vii) notifying the Housing Association of maintenance and repairs needed to the property;

viii) arranging alternative accommodation within a reasonable period of time for tenants whose needs cannot be met at the property. This is likely to be required:

a) if the tenant is inappropriately placed because of his/her need for additional individual support beyond what can be realistically provided, or

b) if a tenant is presenting challenging behaviour which is detrimental to him/herself and/or others, and which creates unsolvable problems within the property;

ix) employing staff to carry out these tasks (Schedule 7).

Example 2

Support Plan

This support plan is central to a floating support scheme which assists people moving from hostels to independent tenancies. Keeping to the support plan is a condition of the tenancy.

Area Identified	Task	By Whom	Timescale	Outcome
The Move Itself	Any assistance?	Referral Agency and work colleagues	Prior to tenancy commencement 31/5	✓
Benefits	To visit DSS in next week (w/k 31/5) to establish benefit entitlement following redundancy on 30/6	Worker at Referral Agency and MsX		Has done ✓
	HB application	Support Worker	–	
	'Unemployed, how to sign on' leaflet	Support Worker	–	Provided ✓
	– Benefit Offices			Provided ✓
Resources of area	To be provided at tenancy sign up	Support Worker	Sign up	✓
	If further info. required, to be requested	Support Worker	As condition	

Continued over...

	Action	Who	When	Status / Notes
Budgeting	Draw up chart detailing disposable income v expenditure. Suggest savings plan in anticipation of bills.	Support Worker	Mid–end–July	Gas/electric meter readings every Wed. when support worker visits
	Provide leaflets re: consumption by different household items and suggest areas of possible economy	Support Worker	ASAP First visit	Provided ✓ (electric only)
	Provide info on Power Key	Support Worker	Before signing up	Provided ✓
Employment	When made redundant (30/6/93), to provide info. on additional employment resources if required	Support Worker	30/6 Upon request	Sickness Benefit (applied for) Wed. 12/7/93 and IS
Move in Day	Read Meters	MsX and workers at Referral Agency	Move in Day	✓ Doing regularly – MsX and support worker
Visits	MsX to maintain regular contact with referral agency. Support worker to visit weekly for first month and then discuss again. If employment gained, meetings to be re-negotiated	MsX and Referral Agency	Weekly for first month	Visited 7/7 but not in. Working? left note. Weekly
		Support Worker	Weekly for first month then review	Weekly
Practical	CH Timer operation Washer dryer (But will be written instructions)	Support Worker Support Worker	Once after move in	When needed ✓

Counselling	To undertake regularly with referral agency	MsX and Referral Agency	Ongoing	✓
Other	Said would like to 'keep occupied'. To discuss how this could best be achieved/facilitated. Perhaps by (a) finding employment – looking (b) evening classes – doing one already, might also join dance theatre	MsX and support worker	Ongoing	Evening/day classes – has chosen to do dance. Is looking for another. Maybe furniture making/soft furnishings/clothes making
Security	Insurance details of Co–op Insurance to be provided	Support Worker	First visit	Social worker to look up local branch in phone book Which? report on insurance Sept. 93 Provided ✓ Ongoing
	Referral agency to provide bleeper for as long as she needs it, in case of emergency	Referral Agency	From tenancy commencement	
Phone	WHICH? article on Telecom v. Mercury to be provided	Support Worker	ASAP	Provided ✓
Keys	To give extra set of keys to referral agency in case of lock out	MsX and Referral Agency	Before move	✓
Employment	To seek it	MsX	When something suitable comes up	Employment gained Nov. 93. Full time senior worker in Care Home

Example 3

A Housing Management Support Specification

This specification has been prepared by an association which provides supportive housing management to single people rehoused in individual tenancies.

Support Needs Degree of Contact	High 2 Visits p/w	Medium 1 Visit p/w	Low Responsive
Liaison with external support services	Refer to and liaise with voluntary & statutory agencies, eg Social Services Mind etc.	Establish need for external agency involvement	n/a
Advice & Information on housing options	Advice at information session and housing interview. Implications of different choices. Counselling to ensure client makes choices that are right for their situation	Advice at information session and housing interview. Implications of different choices. Counselling to ensure client makes choices that are right for their situation	Advice at information session and housing interview. Implications of different choices. Counselling to ensure client makes choices that are right for their situation
Support for independent living	Advice on responsibility for eg rent payment, reporting repairs etc.	Advice on responsibility for eg rent payment, reporting repairs etc.	Advice on responsibility for eg rent payment, reporting repairs etc.
	Facilitate House Meetings in shared housing	Facilitate House Meetings in shared housing	Facilitate House Meetings in shared housing
	Intensive/in–depth counselling on home visits	Responsive counselling on home visits	
Repairs	Assist tenant in identifying necessary repairs	Report to partner HA, arrange access and chase progress	In self contained and floating support: enable tenant to liaise direct with partner housing association with repairs. Chase progress
	Report to partner HA, arrange access and check progress		

Benefits Fuel & Poll Tax	Establish correct entitlement to benefits	Establish correct entitlement to benefits	Establish correct entitlement to benefits
	Monitor payments received to ensure maximum benefit uptake	Monitor payments received to ensure maximum benefit uptake	Monitor payments received to ensure maximum benefit uptake
	Assist client with form filling Arrange for Payment Direct to relevant bodies	Assist client with form filling Arrange for Payment Direct to relevant bodies	Assist client with form filling Arrange for Payment Direct to relevant body
	Advise on establishing budget fuel payment methods if in self contained	Advise on establishing budget fuel payment methods if in self contained	Advise on establishing budget fuel payment methods if in self contained
	Advocate on client's behalf	Advocate on client's behalf	
	Liaison meetings with DSS and HB to minimise administrative arrears		
	Accompany client to office if necessary		
Orientation into a new neighbourhood	Provide Survival Pack & Borough Information Pack	Provide Survival Pack & Borough Information Pack	Provide Survival Pack & Borough Information Pack
	Introduce to other residents & caretaker if appropriate	Introduce to other residents & caretaker if appropriate	Introduce to other residents & caretaker if appropriate
	Identify local facilities to client eg Social Services, Town Hall, Post Office	Identify local facilities to client eg Social Services, Town Hall, Post Office	
	Assist with registration with GP/Health Centre		

Continued over...

Money Management	Advice on money management & domestic budgeting	Advice on money management & domestic budgeting	Advice on money management & domestic budgeting
	Interventionist debt counselling	Advisory debt counselling	
Life Skills Training. (By arrangement with Resettlement Team)	Becoming a tenant	Becoming a tenant	Becoming a tenant
	Dealing with the DSS	Dealing with the DSS	Dealing with the DSS
	Basic DIY skills	Basic DIY skills	Basic DIY skills
	Cooking	Cooking	Cooking
Tenant Participation	Quarterly Newsletter	Quarterly Newsletter	Quarterly Newsletter
	Encourage and build confidence to participate in house meetings	Facilitate house meetings in shared houses	
Facilitation of employment opportunities through GATE & other connections with training providers and potential employers	Mailshot advising of options	Mailshot advising of options	Mailshot advising of options
	Individually tailored intensive counselling, realistic confidence building & motivation	Confidence building & motivation	Motivation
	Mock interview experience	Mock interview experience	
Assistance with gaining move–on accommodation	Arrange move to specialist therapeutic community *or* Refer to Resettlement Team for nomination to independent housing with intensive resettlement support *or* Transfer to floating support scheme/direct managed self–contained housing	Refer to Resettlement Team for nomination to independent housing with medium resettlement support *or* Transfer to Floating Support Scheme direct managed self contained housing	Refer to Resettlement Team for nomination to independent housing with medium/responsive resettlement support

Chapter 4
Specifications

> *'It's a shame but I wonder if there is a cottage industry in producing specifications.'*
> Ross Fraser, quoted in *Housing* July 1993: 24

The intention in this chapter is to provide some background information on the writing of specifications, and then to look at how community care needs might be addressed in the specification process. In order to assist with this process the bulk of the chapter is devoted to detailed consideration of issues which are considered important, and in some cases crucial, in the management of housing for tenants with community care needs.

Existing Guidance

Those authorities which are ahead in the specification process appear to be relying on the writing of their own specifications based on existing procedures, service or business plans, and consultation exercises. Specifications are intended to be available to public view, and for purchase. Authorities seem to be shy of this. A review of specifications is to be published later in 1994 as a joint publication by the Institute, ADC, AMA and CIPFA. Both the ADC, in association with the Institute, and the AMA have produced their own guides to CCT, the latter concentrating on the specification process. The view is taken by these organisations that model specifications are not necessarily helpful as each authority should be preparing them in the light of its own special circumstances.

The AMA has produced a guide to what should be included in specifications in five key topic areas:

- the general introduction
- control and management of empty properties
- rent arrears recovery
- responsive repairs
- neighbour, nuisance and harassment

It also incorporates in an Appendix a fairly comprehensive checklist of topics which could be addressed in specifications, although this might be more useful if it had been divided into the defined activities, and those activities which an authority might wish to include if opting to contract out a more comprehensive service.

Module seven of the ADC/IoH Manual, *Specifying the Housing Service*, pays more attention to the situation where an authority might wish to include non–defined activities. It provides a summary of what should be included in three functional areas:

- rent collection
- tenancy management
- property management

In each case the duties of client and contractor are spelt out, and an indication made of those tasks which might benefit from a procedure based specification. An Annex to the Module provides a sample specification for voids control and for neighbour disputes, examples deliberately chosen to illustrate functions suitable for an output based and procedure based specification. Neither of these publications satisfactorily addresses community care issues although an updated version of the ADC/IoH manual plans to do so. Both draw on the Institute's *Housing Management Standards Manual* which they recommend as a source in relation to procedures and performance. Chapter 12 'Housing Services for People with Special Needs' is of particular relevance for assisting in the specification of services for people with community care needs.

(An additional source which may be helpful in the writing of specifications on neighbour disputes is the Institute's publication *Neighbour Disputes: responses by social landlords*, Karn et al 1993.)

The Output Versus Process Argument

There are two approaches to the writing of specifications. One is to concentrate on the end result; the desired output or desired outcome. These are not the same. Output refers to something which is produced and is often measurable in quantifiable terms, such as numbers of voids, level of arrears. Outcome refers to the result which this output achieves. For example one measure of the output of housing management may be the number of repairs carried out in a certain time period. The outcome will be a better maintained stock and more satisfied tenants. Outcomes can often be more difficult to measure than outputs. Most of the writing on CCT subsumes outcome under output, and since this is a convenient shorthand to use to signify the opposite of the approach in specification writing which concentrates on processes or procedures, this is the practice that will be followed here from this point.

This opposite approach, where specifications are written from the perspective of detailing the processes, or input which must be adopted, is also referred to as the writing of 'tight' as opposed to 'loose' specifications.

Authorities may consider using a mix of approaches, for instance the defined outputs of activities such as voids or rent arrears (eg 2% voids, 3% rent arrears) could be written into the specification, leaving the contractor in the position of providing methods statements as to how such objectives will be attained. In regard to outputs less readily quantifiable, such as neighbour disputes, the authority may wish to specify procedures in detail in order to ensure its policies are adhered to, or may again prefer to let the contractor produce methods statements, outlining the procedures which they propose to adopt.

In its guidance on anti–competitive behaviour the DoE has stated a preference for an output approach, although it has conceded that there are cases where a procedure based specification will be more appropriate. It is, therefore, open to authorities to use such an approach in appropriate areas – such as community care related tasks.

The guidance on CCT specifications by the ADC/IoH (1993/94) and AMA (1994) both seem to take the view that highly prescriptive methods should be viewed with caution for the following reasons:

- the specification needs to be right first time – there is less flexibility for change
- the tenderer's work is done for them – the 'in–house' expertise is given away
- it is more difficult to evaluate the quality of bids
- contractors are less likely to act on their own initiative and suggest improved working methods
- more defaults may be identified which may be costly to investigate but relatively insignificant
- the more onerous the specification the higher the overall cost

The benefits of a tight specification are:

- tenants are more likely to feel that their views have been taken into account
- monitoring is more straightforward
- bids are easier to evaluate because they respond to a uniform set of procedures
- it instils more confidence in the delivery of a quality service
- the authority is more likely to feel its policies will be adhered to

In this context it is interesting to note that Westminster produced tender documents which were extremely prescriptive and very detailed – but nonetheless considered not to be anti–competitive. This is likely to have been a major reason for the withdrawal of three interested housing associations.

Specifying for Community Care

There are three main decisions to be made in specifying for community care:

i) *How to write it*

In the light of the above discussion authorities need to consider whether to adopt the 'tight' or the 'loose' method of covering community care issues in the specifications. In order to protect the interests of community care tenants it appears preferable to ensure that contractors are informed in some detail of requirements in this area rather than being left to set their own procedures. A 'loose' approach may lead to a minimal service, and opportunities to rectify it at a later stage may be limited. If specifications are written in this way it is essential that potential contractors are asked to prepare detailed methods statements on their proposed approaches to community care, and are closely questioned at the interview stage. The methods statements should then be incorporated into a final version of the contract. An advantage of the prescriptive approach is that the standards are then laid down and can be more easily assessed at the monitoring stage.

ii)   *Where to put it*

This concerns whether to include community care issues under each heading of the activities to be contracted out, or to have a separate section on community care, either before or after the body of text on the specifications. To some extent this may relate to what has been included in the general conditions of the contract.

If community care issues are included under the headings for each activity it then becomes more likely that contractors will carry out the specifications in that form for all tenants who would benefit from it, rather than restricting it to community care users. Authorities with a concern for a social and welfare role might therefore prefer this model. It would also be an appropriate model for authorities or areas within an authority with high proportions of community care groups.

The model of a separate section on community care may appeal to authorities which prefer to limit intensive or enhanced housing management only to community care users and/or groups. This model could also be adopted where supported accommodation or specialist services are to be separately packaged. However, authorities should consider if there are any existing examples which could inform the writing of their general specifications.

iii) **What to Put in it**

The content of the specifications relating to community care will reflect the authority's policies and procedures, the needs of existing tenants in community care groups and provision for projected future needs. Given the variety of local circumstances in all these respects it is not possible to write sample specifications that can do justice to the diversity of situations. Authorities need to develop their own specifications which take into account the content of this guide, but are then adapted to their own circumstances. The next section is intended to provide guidelines on ways of addressing the social and welfare issues of housing management which are seen as particularly important in the context of community care.

Specification Checklists

The topics covered include allocations, lettings, tenancy management, rent collection and arrears, repairs and maintenance. For each of these there is a checklist of points which are considered by the authors to be important in the provision of a responsive service to vulnerable tenants. The lists are not intended to be exhaustive and are meant as suggestions to inform the process of writing detailed specifications, or as prompts in expanding on the methods statements required from potential contractors.

Allocations Checklist

☑ An applicant should be visited in his/her existing accommodation.

☑ This visit should look at suitability of present accommodation, likely future needs, coping capacity, financial circumstances support needs etc. – but should *not* judge eg housing standards or risk as a tenant.

☑ A community care assessment should be requested if it appears necessary.

☑ Medical or social reports should be requested where appropriate, and health, social services and other agencies involved contacted.

☑ The ways in which available housing might hinder or help functioning should be assessed.

☑ All available housing options eg sheltered housing, aids and adaptations, move of carer rather than applicant, extra support, should be considered with the applicant, and priorities established.

☑ Reasons for excluding an applicant from the list eg history of arrears, damage to property should be re–examined.

☑ Attention should be paid to stated preferences eg garden/no garden, access, type of heating, cooking system, floor preference.

☑ If rehousing is not immediately available regular checks should be made to see if a change of circumstances might increase priority.

☑ Where discretion is used it should be capable of justification on appeal.

Lettings Checklist

☑ When a vacancy occurs its suitability for a tenant with a community care need should be assessed eg existing adaptations, potential for adaptation.

☑ Suitability of location should be assessed – nearness to shops, access, local transport, environment, balance of community.

☑ The applicant should be visited to discuss an offer.

☑ The applicant should make an accompanied viewing, together with a care manager/key worker, carer or relative where appropriate.

☑ A realistic view of the property should be given, deficiencies in it or the environment should not be glossed over.

☑ Advice should be offered in relation to any necessary repairs etc, and in relation to support which can be offered if it is feared harassment may occur.

☑ If the property is refused the reason should be asked and its applicability to future offers noted.

☑ Refusal should not be used as a reason to impose a penalty such as moving down the list.

☑ If refusals are persistently made social services, carers etc should be consulted about the next step to take.

☑ If the offer is accepted sufficient time needs to be allowed to make necessary support arrangements.

☑ Support needs should be discussed with relevant agencies or individuals.

☑ Any necessary repairs, adaptations should be carried out including decoration if the tenant is unlikely to be able to do it.

☑ Advice and assistance with the removal of furniture, furnishings, connection by services etc, should be offered.

☑ Income should be assessed and advice and assistance with benefit claims given.

☑ A record should be maintained of GP, support worker, next of kin etc.

☑ When the tenant moves in he or she should be accompanied.

☑ The working of all equipment and fixtures should be demonstrated – cooker, central heating, stop taps etc.

☑ The tenancy agreement should be explained.

☑ The tenant should be given information on the local area including shops, public transport, schools, GPs, clinics, libraries etc.

☑ The tenant should be provided with a named contact in case of problems.

☑ The tenant should be visited within two to four weeks to see if there are any problems and to assess if the necessary support is available.

Tenancy Management Checklist

☑ The procedure in relation to breaches of the tenancy agreement (eg damage to property, neglect of garden, rubbish, noise etc) should be as follows:

- – visit the tenant to discuss the issue

- – consider if the breach is serious or petty enough to be overlooked

- – investigate causes and reasons

- – compromise and/or negotiate

- – seek advice and assistance of other agencies (environmental health department, social services)

- – consider realistic sanctions

- – solicitors' letters, notice of seeking possession etc should be final resorts, delivered in person and explained fully

- – eviction should be in extreme cases only and in consultation with care managers/carer etc where available

☑ In cases of neighbour disputes the procedure should be as follows:

- – promote methods of reporting which do not cause intimidation

- – visit both parties to discuss the issue

- – bring both parties together unless it would appear counter–productive

- – consider whether a mediation service would help

- – involve care manager/support worker/carer

- – consider practical solutions eg sound–proofing, fences, increased security

- assess whether what is needed is extra support

- if a transfer is requested investigate whether this would be beneficial, or only move the problem

- legal action should be a last resort

☑ The social environment should aim to provide integration into the community and community support. Methods to achieve this include:

- encouragement of involvement in tenant groups and associations, befriending schemes, lunch clubs, outings etc

- provision of information on local community resources and events

- arrangement of transport to community events

☑ Tenants should be visited regularly with a view to assessing whether they have any problems and whether support plans are operating effectively

☑ Tenants should be offered individual support which could include:

- introduction to neighbours and tenants association
- encouragement to attend community events
- advice and assistance in running the home
- advice and assistance in maintaining the home
- advice on gardening and security
- support with practical matters – shopping, cleaning etc

- support on personal issues – emotional/social/occupational/healthy living

- information and advice on benefits and money management

- advice and assistance on health and medication

(see also Chapter 1)

Rent Collection and Arrears Checklist

☑ In order to minimise rent problems help should be offered to maximise income and claim benefits.

☑ In cases where it seems appropriate assistance should be offered with income and expenditure, referring to a specialist agency if necessary.

☑ Tenants should be encouraged to report if there is any change of circumstance which might affect their income position.

☑ Tenants should be notified of changes in benefit regulations and assistance in understanding them should be offered if requested.

☑ Places where rent payments can be made should be accessible.

☑ A variety of options should be offered in regard to payment methods, and these should be clearly explained.

☑ Door–to–door collections should be considered where this would assist a tenant to make regular payments.

☑ Arrangements for collection of rent by individuals such as wardens, caretakers home helps etc should be considered if this would assist the tenant.

☑ If arrears occur a personal visit should be made after a maximum of two missed payments in order to establish the reason.

☑ At this visit any changes which affect income and benefit levels should be investigated.

☑ Individual circumstances rather than the size of the debt should direct what action is taken.

☑ Standardised letters should be avoided if possible, and if used should be delivered by hand and explained. The distress such letters may cause should not be underestimated.

☑ Social workers, support workers, carers etc should be kept informed of the situation.

☑ Arrears should not be used as a reason for withholding repairs or delaying transfer requests etc.

☑ Repayment arrangements should be realistic, taking into account the extra living costs certain tenants may have to bear.

☑ Eviction should be considered only as a last resort and after consultation with relevant agencies.

☑ An eviction should not take place until alternative accommodation has been found.

☑ Former tenants should not be pursued for arrears without due consideration to the effect this may have, and where appropriate consultation with relevant agencies.

Repairs and Maintenance Checklist

☑ Visits at regular intervals should establish whether there is a need for any repairs, with particular attention paid to tenants whose capabilities in noticing and reporting repairs are uncertain.

☑ At tenancy take–up the function and operation of equipment such as central heating alarms, stop cocks, fuse boxes etc should be demonstrated.

☑ A list of common problems should be provided with a checklist of the steps a tenant can take, either to remedy the problems or whom to contact. Particular attention should be drawn to identifying and acting on emergency situations such as gas leaks.

☑ Recognition should be given to the fact that otherwise straightforward matters such as changing a light bulb, fitting a plug, understanding instructions, bending and reaching, may prove difficult for some tenants. Arrangements should be made to address this.

☑ Reporting systems should be as simple as possible and where necessary tailored for individual needs, eg freephone systems, pre–paid cards, reporting by home helps etc, reporting through an emergency alarm system.

☑ Individuals taking repairs reports should be trained to be reassuring, to assess when a real emergency has arisen and to deal with panic anxiety and paranoia.

☑ The record system should identify those tenants who might be vulnerable if repairs are not carried out promptly.

☑ Repairs should be prioritised by the needs of the individual rather then the category of repair eg a heating breakdown may be an emergency for an elderly or disabled tenant.

☑ In defining an emergency a wide definition of danger to health and safety should be used which includes anxiety and stress factors.

☑ If there is any uncertainty about the nature of the repair or the ability of the tenant to report accurately a visit should be made.

☑ The upset caused by a repair should not be underestimated. This may lead to the decision to decant temporarily. Where necessary relevant agencies should be consulted.

☑ Before the repair takes place the tenant should be visited to explain what will be done and how long it will take.

☑ Contractors for the repair should be warned of potential problems eg possibility that services must be disconnected all day, that the tenant may not be able to move or protect furniture themselves, that constant noise may be stressful, that extra care in tidying up and storing tools may be necessary.

☑ If a choice of fittings, colours etc is offered advice should be given where necessary.

☑ The appropriateness of offering redecoration allowances should be assessed and where necessary arrangements should be made for the work to be done.

☑ After the work is completed the tenant should be visited to see if there are any problems and if the operation of any new equipment etc is understood.

☑ The planned maintenance programme should include regular inspection and servicing of lifts, heating systems cooling systems, alarm services etc.

☑ If maintenance works are to take place the tenant should be visited, the implications explained and the tenant's ability to cope assessed.

☑ Where necessary relevant agencies should be consulted, particularly if the tenant may have to be decanted.

☑ Consideration should be given as to whether the tenant's particular circumstances warrant his or her exclusion from a planned programme of work, or justify the need for a one–off job to minimise disruption and delay.

☑ If there is a 'menu' system of improvements in operation the tenant may need advice and assistance on what to choose.

☑ Occupational therapists etc should be consulted on suitability of work for the needs of the tenant, and the opportunity taken to include any 'extras' where possible.

Extracts from the Institute's Housing Management Standards Manual
Chapter 12 *Housing Services for People with Special Need*

These extracts are included to illustrate the style and content of the standards which the Institute feels should be taken into account in order to reflect the particular requirements of tenants with community care needs.

16 Rent collection, accounting and arrears recovery

16.1 Deal sensitively with tenants who are in rent arrears, because of matters related to their special needs such as ill health, mental infirmity, personal crisis.

16.2 Ensure that older tenants and tenants with serious physical or mental health problems are not sent inappropriate threatening letters for technical or small arrears.

16.3 Ensure that rent payment options are accessible and convenient for people with special needs, for example, provide door–to–door collection services where appropriate.

16.4 Have an agreed strategy with social service authorities and other relevant agencies for dealing with the arrears of tenants who have special needs which make them less able to manage their financial affairs and to cope with repossession procedures and eviction.

16.5 Liaise with the housing benefit section to help to ensure that tenants with special needs promptly receive their correct housing benefit entitlement.

17 Repairs and Maintenance

17.1 Have arrangements for reporting repairs which are simple for people with special needs to use.

17.2 Ensure that maintenance records identify tenants with special needs.

17.3   Carry out regular maintenance and safety inspections in the homes of tenants who are unable to identify repair faults, for example, because of visual impairments or learning difficulties.

17.4   Set shorter than normal repair response times for households with vulnerable people where they are less able to cope with the defect or where the defect may put them at risk, for example, heating repairs for older people.

17.5   Take into account the tenant's particular special needs when specifying repairs, for example, specify tap handles suitable for older people.

17.6   Carry out simple repair tasks that are normally the landlord's responsibility such as changing electric fuses, where tenants' special needs prevent them from doing the work themselves.

17.7   Minimise the inconvenience caused to tenants with special needs, because of repairs and maintenance works by helping them to prepare for jobs, cope with works whilst in progress and deal with the after effects, for example:

   • give adequate notice of works and their effects such as disrupted water or fuel supply
   • move furniture, lift carpets and protect furniture
   • take extra care in cleaning up
   • notify care and support agencies as needed.

17.8   Consider decanting people with special needs whilst repairs are carried out where the work is likely to affect their mental or physical health or cause them undue inconvenience.

17.9   Ensure that decanting arrangements for tenants with special needs take account of their housing, care and support requirements and are made in consultation with the agencies providing such services.

17.10   Assistant tenants with special needs who are unable to decorate their homes because of old age or physical or mental infirmity by, for example, providing or arranging internal decoration services.

Sample of Detailed Specifications

These examples of detailed specifications, one in relation to allocations and the other in relation to tenancy management, are intended to serve as possible ways of incorporating community care issues in the contract specification. They are not intended to be complete and self–contained, nor are they necessarily expected to be adopted in their present form. Each authority needs to consider firstly whether they are useful or appropriate in relation to their own local circumstances and, secondly how they might fit in with other parts of the contract documentation.

The Rehousing Assessment Process

Although written in terms of specification for CCT this example embraces good practice which could equally be adopted where allocations is retained on the client side.

1.1   The Contractor shall ensure that staff engaged in rehousing assessment have relevant training in regard to community care legislation, the authority's community care policies, priorities and procedures, and the necessary skills for interviewing people with community care needs. This will include the ability to recognise whether applicants have support needs which have hitherto been unidentified. In addition the Contractor shall ensure that staff have an awareness of what constitutes suitable housing for various community care needs, and of the availability of such housing in the local area.

1.2   The Contractor shall at all times ensure that an applicant is assisted to identify and articulate his or her needs through the presence of a care manager, key worker, advocate, interpreter, carer, relative, friend or other person, as appropriate to the circumstances. Such person shall also be party to any decisions made with or on behalf of the applicant.

1.3   Where an applicant for rehousing has come through a community care route this will normally be apparent to the Contractor as a referral will either have come through the client side services or directly from the referral agency. In such cases the rehousing need will be deemed to be part of a care package relating to the individual's situation as determined at the community care assessment.

1.4   Where an individual application for rehousing suggests any possibility that the applicant might fall into one of the community care groups defined by the social services authority the Contractor shall advise the applicant of his or her right to a community care assessment.

1.5   Where the applicant agrees to a community care assessment the Contractor, shall, in accordance with the relevant procedures, request the relevant department to consider whether a community care assessment is appropriate.

1.6   Where a community care assessment is carried out the Contractor shall where possible arrange to be present, and to attend any case conference arising from the assessment. Such attendance will assist the Contractor to establish how the housing need relates to other aspects of the applicant's care. Where attendance is not possible the Contractor shall liaise with the care manager in order to establish all relevant facts of the case.

1.7   Where the relevant department considers that a community care assessment is not required the Contractor shall not conclude that the duty to consider the community care needs of the applicant is thereby discharged but shall continue to take into account any requirements the applicant may have which can be met by rehousing in a particular setting, by the particular attributes of a property, or by a particular form of housing management support.

1.8   Whether in the context of a joint community care assessment with a care manager or a rehousing assessment by the Contractor alone, the present accommodation of the applicant shall be visited, if necessary on more than one occasion, and the applicant interviewed, in order to establish the nature of any housing and support needs.

1.9   At this interview and any subsequent interview the Contractor shall address the following issues:

•   what existing needs the current accommodation is able to meet

- what existing needs the current accommodation is not able to meet
- what alternatives and options are available

1.10   In addressing this information the Contractor shall endeavour to have available all existing housing records for the applicant and such other records as can be obtained from agencies which have, or have had, any responsibility for the care of the applicant.

1.11   At the interview the Contractor shall have regard to the applicant's physical, mental/emotional, and social/coping abilities.

Matters relating to physical capabilities shall be assessed in relation to for example:

- mobility
- other physical disability
- sensory impairment (sight, hearing)
- general health and presence of acute, chronic, degenerative or progressive illness.

The Contractor shall not rely solely on the applicant's evaluation of his/her condition but take into account existing records and observations of, for example, ability to cross the room, manage steps unaided.

Matters relating to mental/emotional capabilities shall be assessed in relation to for example:

- confusion
- depression
- anxiety
- learning difficulties
- dementia
- mental health problems
- addictions

Matters relating to social/coping capabilities shall be assessed in relation to for example:

- managing the home

- managing shopping etc.
- managing finances
- managing personal care

In all these matters the Contractor is not expected to arrive at a detailed diagnosis, but in association with available records, and where necessary by calling on specialist assistance, draw out the rehousing and housing management implications of the applicant's capabilities. The interview is in no way to be used as a merit test or basis for a system of grading as to suitability as a tenant.

1.12 The Contractor shall assess the presence and adequacy of existing support arrangements both home–based, for example home help, district nurse, informal carer, formal care, residential warden, mobile warden, alarm service etc, and community based, for example day care, respite care, clinic or hospital out patient services. In assessing level of support the Contractor shall have regard to the needs expressed by the applicant, the opinion of the provider, and of any other person involved with the care of the applicant.

1.13 The Contractor shall discuss with the applicant all available housing and support options, describing in detail what the Contractor might be able to offer in accommodation managed by the Contractor and suggesting to which other, if any, agents the applicant might apply for further information.

1.14 Where it appears that the applicant might remain in existing accommodation managed by the Contractor if more support were to be offered, the Contractor shall consider whether and in what way such additional support might be achieved, liaising where necessary with social services, the health authority and voluntary organisations. This may include requesting a review of a community care plan.

1.15 After due consideration of all the circumstances the contractor shall engage in a process of negotiation with the applicant at which the next step in the application is decided. This will determine whether the applicant will remain in the present accommodation managed by the contractor, whether he or she will be accepted on to the rehousing list, or whether he or she will remain housed or be rehoused by another agency.

1.16 Where the applicant is to remain in the accommodation managed by the Contractor, the Contractor shall follow relevant procedures to ensure that any necessary improvements, adaptations or support are provided.

1.17 Where the applicant is to be placed on the rehousing list the Contractor shall follow the relevant procedures to ensure that agencies responsible for the provision of any necessary adaptations and support will be able to do so at such time as a suitable property becomes available. The Contractor shall also establish with the applicant the precise nature of the applicant's preferences and willingness to compromise where the ideal solution cannot be reached. For instance if the preferred option is a bungalow with an alarm system and a mobile warden in a desired area, would the applicant consider accepting a flat in a high rise sheltered scheme with a resident warden in a less desired area?

1.18 Where the applicant is to be referred to another agency for rehousing the Contractor shall ensure that a personal contact is established with that agency, if such contact is not already in existence, and that the applicant's case is furthered at the earliest possible time.

1.19 Where the Contractor is unable to offer a suitable property immediately, liaison shall be maintained with the applicant over the progress of the application, with contact made at a maximum of six week intervals. In addition the applicant shall be advised to report at any time any change of circumstance which might affect his or her housing situation.

Tenant Welfare (Tenants in Mainstream Housing)

1.1 The Contractor shall ensure that each tenant who is a community care user or who is identified as having a community care need is visited at a minimum of every 3 months. Such tenants will be notified to the Contractor by the client.

1.2   In addition, such other tenants as are notified to the Contractor
       by the Client shall be visited at more regular intervals and for
       such purposes as are further specified by the Client.

1.3   Where the tenant is the subject of a community care plan the
       Contractor shall familiarise him or herself with the nature of that
       plan, where necessary liaising with the relevant agency.

1.4   In the course of a visit to a tenant who is the subject of a
       community care plan the Contractor shall enquire of the tenant
       and/or his or her carer/advocate/relative whether the care plan is
       operating to the satisfaction of the tenant, and if not, which
       aspects are unsatisfactory. The Contractor shall then liaise with
       the care manager to endeavour to resolve any problem. A report
       shall be sent to the Client as to the steps taken and any
       difficulties arising.

1.5   Where the tenant is notified to the Contractor as having a
       community care need the Contractor shall familiarise himself or
       herself with any care and support arrangements in relation to
       that tenant, where necessary by contacting the relevant agency or
       individual. In the course of a visit to such a tenant the Contractor
       shall discover if such arrangements are operating to the
       satisfaction of the tenant. If this is not the case the Contractor
       shall liaise with the relevant agency or individual. Where no
       satisfactory resolution is arrived at the Contractor shall report to
       the client.

1.6   Where the Contractor, in the course of a routine visit to a tenant
       who is neither a community care user nor known to have any
       existing community care needs, identifies that a tenant might fall
       into one of the community care groups listed in the general
       conditions to the Contract, then the Contractor shall notify the
       Client, according to the procedural guidelines stated in the
       general conditions to the Contract.

1.7   In the course of a visit to a community care user, or to a tenant
       with community care needs, the Contractor shall, in addition to
       assessing the satisfactory operation of any care plan, or care and
       support arrangement, use his or her own observation and
       discussion with the tenant and his or her carer or advocate to
       establish whether in the opinion of the Contractor or the tenant

or both, there are any problems in relation to the following issues:

- the general external environment – arising for instance from access to the property, lighting, traffic, dogs, litter, graffiti, noise

- the internal environment – house design and layout, ability to understand the functioning of and/or to use equipment and fixtures etc

- maintenance of the property – eg decorating, gardening, cleaning, simple repairs such as changing light bulbs

- performance of daily living tasks – shopping, laundry, preparation of meals, personal cleanliness

- the contracting of and negotiating with agencies such as DSS, social services, gas, electricity and water companies, advice agencies etc

- neighbour relations – harassment, victimisation, taunting, avoidance of contact

- socialisation – awareness of community groups and events, limitations in attending these, receiving visitors (family and friends)

- occupation – especially where the tenant is not in employment

- personal well–being – emotional and mental condition

- physical health

  In assessing these issues the Contractor is not expected to make a detailed diagnosis but to gain an overall impression. The Contractor shall clearly explain to the tenant that the intention is not to make judgements but to enable the tenant to sustain the tenancy.

1.8   Where the tenant is discovered to have problems relating to any of the issues at 1.7 above, or in any other matter which the Contractor feels affects the tenant's ability to sustain the tenancy, then the Contractor, in discussion with the tenant, his or her care manager, or carer, or advocate, shall consider how such problems might be resolved. These may include consideration of the following:

- the provision of aids, adaptations or improvements, or rehousing advice

- ways to resolve cases of neighbour nuisance and harassment etc

- the provision or organisation of assistance with property maintenance and daily living tasks

- the contacting of agencies and individuals on the tenant's behalf

- the provision of information on, and the arranging of assistance with attending local community events

- introduction to neighbours

- the seeking of specialist assistance in regard to physical or mental state of health.

1.9   The Contractor shall consider whether there might be a need for the tenant to be referred for a community care assessment, or a review of a community care plan. The Contractor shall liaise with the Client over such cases.

1.10   Where the Contractor is of the opinion that the problems of a tenant who is not to be considered for a community care assessment could in whole or in part be resolved by the provision of additional support to the tenant, which the Contractor is not, by nature of the Contract, expected to provide, then the Contractor shall explore all available options to ensure such support is provided for the tenant.

1.11   The Contractor shall not make any arrangements in regard to paras 1.8, 1.9 or 1.10 without prior discussion with the tenant, and the seeking of his or her agreement, or that of his or her carer or advocate. It shall be clearly explained to the tenant that the intention is primarily to enable the tenant to sustain the tenancy, and to promote the tenant's welfare.

1.12 The Contractor shall make a written report of each visit to a tenant who is a community care user or who has a community care need, the purpose of which will be to highlight any problems, make suggestions for their resolution and list any steps taken to secure such resolution. This report shall provide the basis for the discussion at any subsequent visit. The Contractor shall make any such report available to the Client on request.

Chapter 5
The Pilot Experience

> '*What has been gained? The knowledge that housing management
> services in deprived East London are as competent as any. The
> proof that local authorities can take on the competition.*'
> *Inside Housing* 1994:9

Housing management is the only public service subject to CCT for which
the government has agreed to allow pilot schemes. The intention of this
is for authorities to learn from the experience gained during the
process, drawing on what might prove to be the strengths and avoiding
the weaknesses. However, in the event this has proved of limited value
as the majority of authorities will have to let contracts before
meaningful evaluative information from the pilots is available.

The pilot authorities are:

- Westminster LBC
- Brent LBC
- Newham LBC
- Rochdale MBC
- Mansfield DC
- Derby City Council
- Mid Suffolk DC
- East Staffs DC

These authorities represent a diversity of stock size and type, from
inner city to scattered rural area. The fact that each has taken a
different approach underlines the fact that there is no single way in

which CCT of housing management can be pursued, and that each authority must take into account its local circumstances.

Detailed research into the pilot authorities has been hampered by the dearth of information they are willing to release. In some a veil of secrecy appears to have been drawn due to the feeling of threat engendered by the competition process. However information, if somewhat incomplete, has been made available from two of the pilot authorities in regard to CCT and their approach to community care issues. The two accounts are provided in the belief that they offer some information which can serve to highlight the potential choices and strategies.

Case Study 1

The authority originally planned to let its first contract in October 1994 but this has now been abandoned. The intention is to have a 'dummy run' on the contract estate, with a selection exercise to be carried out in March 1994, and the service run under contract conditions from April. A select list of tenderers will be compiled in April 1994, with contracts to be let in the Autumn of 1995, and in operation in April 1996.

Community Care

The authority has a commitment to meeting the housing needs of those it defines as having special needs. These include:

- people with physical disabilities
- people with learning difficulties
- people with mental health needs
- elderly people
- lesbians and gay men
- black and Asian people
- women
- young people

There are in existence a number of partnerships and agreements with other statutory agencies and voluntary organisations. There has been a post of special needs officer for six years, and this person has been active in the formulation of the community care plan and in joint planning with health and social services for particular client groups. Relationships with other departments and agencies have been built up which are based on a network of personal contacts and an avoidance of formalised procedures.

Preparation for CCT

In preparing for CCT, the authority believes that tenants should receive a service which is:

- high quality
- comprehensive
- caring but firm
- customer centred
- accountable
- effectively monitored
- value for money

A service policy statement has been prepared which sets out the objectives, concerns and requirements for the housing service in the CCT context. It aims to express the philosophy behind the borough's policies and strategies, in order to inform both the contract documentation and the potential contractors.

The document makes it clear that the contractor is required to provide a service which is friendly, courteous, sensitive, responsive, and accepting of individual difference, although this is phrased in terms of generalities. There is little to suggest that housing management might have a social and welfare function which contractors need to address, nor is community care mentioned. However, there is a statement on equal opportunities and provision for special needs.

> *'The service will at all times be alert to the special needs of particular groups of clients and, within the contract, make special provision in terms of staffing, facilities and training to ensure that these needs are met.'*

Client/Contractor Split

The authority has determined upon a 'soft' split at Assistant Director level. Each of five Assistant Directors will act as a 'local client' responsible for the 5 townships into which the borough is divided. Three of these Assistant Directors will have housing management responsibilities on the contractor side as well. This will require careful accounting of CCT and non–CCT activities in order for activities to be charged correctly. The advantages of this form of split are seen as:

* maintaining a comprehensive service
* staff flexibility
* monitoring is made easier
* a 'hard' split might result in 'camps' with community care clients falling between them

The post of special needs officer will remain on the client side.

Packaging

The contracts will be divided between the five geographical areas or townships, with the contractors using the five existing area offices. The activities to be contracted out are the defined activities with the addition of allocations. The intention is for housing management to be generic with no specialist posts on the contractor side. It appears that the special needs officer (client side) will remain responsible for taking referrals of tenants with community care needs, and will nominate them to the contractor where relevant.

Contract Specification

The contract specification runs to some 500 pages, and has involved two people working full time for almost a year. Before writing began the process was discussed with other departments with experience of CCT. Rewriting was undertaken after consultation and checking, clause by clause, with Union representatives. The tenants' federation has had a representative on the steering group for the process, which has involved fortnightly meetings. The specification is divided into the defined activities as set out by the DoE, with the addition of allocations. There is also a general section, and one on contract conditions. The final version should be produced in March 1994.

There is a strong belief that allocations are the crucial aspect in the housing service, and the section of the specification on allocations is as much as the rest put together. This section specifies exactly what the contractors will be required to do, and at the tender evaluation stage they will have to show how it will be achieved. Other sections such as rent collection, are specified on an output basis, with the contractor expected to show how targets will be met. Possibilities for variation in the contract are dealt within the text of the specification. For example, there is a policy that in certain cases, particularly for people in sheltered housing, rent should be collected at the door, if requested. The contractor has to accept that these numbers may increase at the request of the client officer, either at his or her discretion, or if approached by social services.

Community care has been addressed in two ways within the specification. Firstly, it has been referred to where appropriate under each defined activity, and secondly, there is a short section entitled 'Care in the Community'. With regard to the former, there is little opportunity to comment, since it has not been possible to see more than a few pages of the draft specification. Where relevant, for instance in adaptations for the physically disabled, it has been made clear that the contractor must liaise with social services, although detailed procedures are not described. It appears that the community care aspect of housing management is one area which will be looked for in the methods statements which contractors are to provide in tendering for the contract. It is felt that the nature of the service to people with community care needs is highly dependent upon the outlook, ethos and aims of the individuals and organisations providing that service. By asking for methods statements this may assist in assessing these factors in potential contractors. Further, such methods statements will then be incorporated into the contract, subject to pre–contract negotiations. The intention is that this will lead more easily to compliance from the contractor, since part of the contract specification will thus have been determined by the contractor.

The two page section on care in the community outlines the council's commitment to the policy, and the importance of enabling people to live in their own homes where at all possible. It states:

'Recipients of community care services include older people, people with mental health problems, people with learning difficulties, disabled people, people who are HIV or who have Aids, women who have suffered violence at home, people with drink, drug or other substance related problems and children with special needs.'

The contractor is required to comply with the council's policy on community care, be familiar with the Community Care Plan 'Working Together', respect the confidentiality of care users, and in no way discriminate against community care users. In regard more specifically to working practices there are three clauses which state:

- the contractor will work co–operatively with, and assist all those involved with community care assessments and care managers

- the contractor will ensure that all aspects of the specified service are adjusted where necessary to meet the particular needs of care service users and carers

- the contractor will attend any meeting requested by a care manager at 12 hours notice. The meetings being up to three hours duration and numbering up to 10 per year.

Case Study 2

This authority intends to have its contracts operational in April 1996, although it may decide to invoke the exemption window in regard to local government reorganisation if the pace of implementation becomes too hectic.

Community Care

A new post of community care manager has been created which is located in the services division. This person is to be the focal point for all community care issues, acting as a gatekeeper and central referral point as well as the key person in identifying housing and community care needs for the area, and liaising with other relevant agencies. Arrangements are not yet in place for involvement in community care assessments.

The housing department has taken the initiative in setting up a housing forum, chaired by housing, and with representatives from social services, the health authority and the voluntary sector. The aim is to formulate a co–ordinated housing and community care strategy for the city, addressing in particular new build requirements and the need for adaptations and improvements.

Preparation for CCT

A clear strategy has been developed in regard to the CCT process, based on detailed exploration and planning of all the issues.

A business plan, containing the aims and objectives for the housing service for the period 1993/96 has been drawn up, although this is not specifically related to the CCT process. It covers stock condition, housing need, customer care, housing and the environment, housing and the economy, and community care.

The objectives for community care are identified as:

1. to research and identify community care needs, plan for their provision and develop an initial 'care' strategy

2. to review the lifeline service (alarm call system) and expand it to respond to the care needs of elderly people

3. to explore the feasibility of providing a private sector mobile warden service

4. to explore the feasibility of extending the lifeline service to households with community care needs but who are not elderly

5. to develop a housing starter pack for schools, to educate young people about housing issues

6. to explore the availability of health authority finance to support the development of a joint housing with care project with the Health Authority

7. to explore the feasibility of decentralising the adaptation service for disabled people in the public sector

8. to set up an adaptations register for the public and private social housing sector to maximise best use of stock and enable better targeting of existing adapted dwellings to people in need

Client/Contractor Split

In preparation for CCT the housing department has reorganised its previous 5 divisions into 3 as follows:

Contract Management
Defined housing management activity
Defined housing maintenance activity
DSO support services, eg administration, personnel
Financial management

Policy and Strategy
Housing policy formulation
Client side housing management contract control

Client side housing maintenance contract control
Research and enabling role
Client side administrative support including information technology
Financial control
Property sales (including Right to Buy and Rent to Mortgage)

Housing Services
Housing functions either exempt or not yet subject to CCT and provided primarily to private sector customers.
Urban renewal
Grant administration/Home Aid Agency
Pre–tenancy housing services including exempt activity
Houses in multiple occupation management
Community care/Central Control services

The duties of staff have been redefined so that no–one below Director level has responsibilities combining client and contractor functions. This 'hard' split is in direct contrast to the authority in Case Study 1.

Packaging

The stock of over 17,000 is to be packaged into 11 contracts one for each local housing area, with no more than 2000 homes in each.

The authority is committed to the retention of the existing comprehensive and integrated service and is therefore including some non–defined functions in the contracts – such as, for example, allocations.

A problem has arisen in relation to the Housing Options Service (a one–stop shop) which combines exempt, non–defined and defined activities such as homelessness, nominations, assessments and home visits. It is felt that it is essential to maintain this service in its current form, and it is therefore anticipated that the 'exempt proportion' will be used to retain on the client side those aspects of this service which are defined activities.

Less problematic is the position of the current money advice service. Money advice is not a defined activity but it is closely related to arrears, which is. The decision has been that a voluntary agreement will be entered into with the contractor which will give the contractor managerial responsibility, but with existing staff seconded to (and therefore paid by) the contractor. The service will however, remain under the control of the client. The contract specifications will state at what stage the contractor must hand over to the money advice service.

It is for the client side to determine how the housing service will be run, and the contractor will be expected to have the skills and employ the staff which are considered necessary to deliver that service. This includes the provision of such social and welfare functions as the authority offers its tenants. For example there is an existing post of housing visitor (the only non–generic post) whose main function is to visit each tenant once a year for 20 minutes. The housing visitor has multi–functional training and uses the occasion to find out if the tenant has any problems, to take repairs reports, offer welfare benefits advice, conduct customer surveys and check on service delivery. The contractor will be expected to provide a member of staff to fulfil this function in precisely the same way.

The 11 housing management contracts start with base specifications. Beyond this tenants can to a certain extent choose the level of service they wish. This follows the existing system where tenants can opt for local conditions of tenancy, which can simply be a ban on keeping dogs, or the option to include extra services such as resident caretakers, contract cleaning or garden maintenance. Such services are subject to a rent add–on, which is eligible for housing benefit. (The Director was at pains to point out that this did not result in tenants on housing benefit opting for all available extras. On the contrary there was a concern to strike a balance in order to keep rent levels reasonable, since there is a commitment by the majority to be in a position to discontinue having to claim benefits.)

Sheltered housing is to be included in general contracts to encourage a feeling of integration into the community. The overriding priority has been to retain continuity of services to older people. The property, or bricks and mortar side, will be managed by the contractor, whilst the care side will be the subject of a voluntary management agreement (in the same way as the money advice service described above). Wardens will in effect be seconded to the contractor whilst the client controls the nature of their work. At the end of the contract period the wardens will revert back to the client and be available for a new contract.

A recently established respite care service is run under a joint planning agreement with social services, which funds full time care staff. Under CCT this arrangement will continue, with the contractor taking responsibility for the property side, as above.

The central control and mobile warden system will be retained under a service level agreement, and will not be part of the housing management contract. The contractor will be informed that certain tenants are linked to the central control.

Contract Specification

The preambles (general conditions) to the contract will state the framework of the contract, for example the requirement that the contractor must accept the performance of certain non–defined activities in order to gain the contract. The specifications are function not output specific and based on existing procedures manuals which cover all aspects of the housing service. They are written on a step by step basis which makes clear how the contractor is to proceed in any eventuality, with the intention of avoiding the situation where the contractor might claim additional costs for unanticipated circumstances. Penalties for non–compliance are built into the documentation.

The approach to community care in the contract documentation is driven by the consideration that conditions should not arise which call on any extra input in housing management terms.

Anyone discharged into the community from an institution must have a care package in place before being rehoused. This will take the form of a contract with the referring agency who will be expected to be responsible for the care. The care package will become a part of the conditions of tenancy, and if not adhered to will constitute a breach of tenancy. So for instance if a schizophrenic does not take the prescribed medication he or she could be evicted. Any additional housing management costs incurred because care is not delivered as arranged must be quantified by the contractor, and charged as a default on the care contract.

The community care manager will be responsible for assessing whether community care packages have been adequately drawn up, and for monitoring their effectiveness. This will rely on exceptional cases reporting from the contractor.

For those already in the community and not subject to a community care assessment but whom the contractor may deem to have community care needs, there will be a requirement to follow specified procedures in referring to other agencies. These procedures are laid out in a technical annex. If the referral agency refuse to accept a community care need and the tenant is presenting housing management problems, then if necessary grounds for eviction would be sought eg nuisance.

Conclusions from Case Studies

The approaches of these authorities to both community care and CCT have been very different. Case study 1 has had a commitment over the last few years to address the housing requirements of those tenants whom it considers to have special needs. The special needs officer has established a network of personal relationships based on informal procedures with other agencies concerned in the provision of support and care. The relatively *ad hoc* way this has been pursued is reflected in the 'loose' way the issue of community care is approached in the CCT framework. The advantage of this is that it allows for flexibility and sensitivity in dealing with individual community care cases – although it may depend on the goodwill of the contractor to deliver this responsive sort of service.

Cases study 2 has only recently addressed the issue of community care and its significance for housing. The approach is based on the businesslike and commercial culture of the organisation and this is reflected in the 'tight' nature of CCT specifications and the emphasis on the adherence to rigid procedures. This emphasis is likely to result in an inflexible and stereotypical approach which could all to easily lead to the eviction of vulnerable tenants – who may still have to be rehoused under current legislation.

There are a number of points arising from the approach of these authorities which might inform the thinking of others when addressing community care in the CCT process. These can be divided into certain topics.

Client Side Responsibilities

- Given that most authorities are likely to retain a responsibility for community care on the client side it seems crucial that they become involved in care assessments and the preparation of care packages – especially where (as in Case Study 2) they are expected to make judgements about what constitutes a satisfactory care package.

- Given that rehousing is such a crucial factor in the operation of satisfactory care, all authorities need to examine how to protect community care tenants where allocation is to be contracted out.

Case Study 1 has determined on retaining allocations for such tenants on the client side but may face problems in maintaining the existing relationship based on goodwill. It is unclear how Case Study 2 will address this issue.

Definition of Terms

- At the outset there should be a definition of the terms, often interchangeably used, of community care user, community care clients, community care groups, special needs groups, people with community care needs.

- There needs to be a clear distinction between those who have had a community care assessment, and those who have a community care need, and how this might affect how the contractor responds to them.

- Community care needs is taken as an umbrella term which may need clarification in certain places in the contract documentation – should the service be 'adjusted' (Case Study 1) in the same way for the needs of an elderly person as for a person with alcohol problems.

Procedures

- Liaison arrangements with the client side officer responsible for community care need to be detailed: for example in what circumstances and at what stage must the client side be informed of particular situations.

- Precise guidelines need to be given on how the contractor is to identify a tenant with a community care need.

- Precise guidelines need to be given to the contractor in regard to the monitoring of whether a care package is effective or not.

- Some reference needs to be made to the different procedures that might need to be followed where tenants have different levels of support – ranging from a neighbour coming in once a week, to a full package of care.

Specification

- A consistent approach needs to be adopted. Case Study 2 has attempted to cover all eventualities, and removes the potential of the contractor to use initiative and show a 'human' face. It does, however, mean that the client controls how the service should be delivered. Case Study 1 vacillates between being extremely vague ('adjusting the service where necessary'), and extremely specific ('meetings of three hours duration 10 times a year' – can this be guaranteed?). By relying on potential contractors' methods statements the risk is that the approach to community care issues will be contractor, not client–led.

Conclusion

This conclusion aims to draw out the main points discussed in the text in order to highlight key areas in relation to housing management, community care and CCT.

■ Housing authorities need to accept that housing has a key role to play in community care, and that this extends beyond the physical provision of a house. It is crucial for authorities to become involved in the joint planning process with social services and health authorities, and to participate in meaningful dialogue in the assessment process. If effective co-ordination is achieved at all stages many housing management problems may be avoided.

■ For those tenants with community care needs in mainstream housing, the housing management service should offer more than a minimal 'bricks and mortar' landlord role. The extent to which the aspects of the social role, defined in Chapter 1, are undertaken will depend on the philosophy of the service, the perceived needs of the local area, the available resources and the expressed wishes of the users. Agreement on a division of responsibilities for particular tasks should be made with other agencies involved, particularly social services authorities.

■ Authorities may decide that the sort of responsive and sensitive housing management that some vulnerable tenants need is best provided through specialist posts, which within the framework of CCT, could be kept on the client side. An alternative is to include the social role in a generic service which is contracted out. A third approach would be to contract out a specialist service separate from the main housing management contract. The choice made will depend on local circumstances including the skills of potential tenderers.

■ In preparing for CCT an authority must first scrutinise its existing service, and examine where improvements can be made. The cost implications of the various options should be considered. It can then move on to consider what type of service it wishes to provide in the future, and how this can be formulated into a strategy which can inform the CCT process.

■ Central decisions relate to the extent to which housing management activities will be contracted out, the division of responsibilities between client and contractor, and the way in which the service is packaged. In addition, it is necessary to consider at this stage what criteria will be used to select the contractor, how bids will be evaluated, how performance will be assessed, and how variation in the contract will be addressed. Within each of these decision areas the requirements of, and consequences for, tenants with community care needs must be considered. Understanding of this will be informed by ensuring that such tenants are identified and included at all stages of the tenant consultation process.

■ The achievement of community care objectives should be a consideration at every stage in the preparation of the contract documentation. The framework within which the actual contract specifications are to operate must be precise and clear to ensure that the whole contract is rigorous and internally consistent. This is particularly important in the community care context in relation to statements which describe the authority's community care policies, the requirements for the type of service which is to be delivered, the liaison procedures with other agencies, and the arrangements for involvement in assessments, care plans, and the provision of support.

■ The community care implications of each activity need to be addressed in the specification, either by describing detailed procedures, or by ensuring that the methods statements of contractors adequately cover all the issues.

■ It cannot be overstressed that it is at the stage of contract documentation, and in particular the writing of specifications, that the future nature of the housing management service will be determined, and that omissions or oversights may crucially affect the ability of tenants with community care needs to have these needs met and perhaps to sustain their tenancy.

References

ADC/IoH (1993)
Competition and Local Authority Housing Services: a Guidance Manual,
London: ADC/IoH

Arnold, P., Bochel, H., Brodhurst, S. and Page, D. (1991)
Community Care: The Housing Dimension, York: Joseph Rowntree
Foundation

Arnold, P. and Page, D. (1992)
Bricks and Mortar or Foundation for Action, Hull: Humberside
Polytechnic

Association of Metropolitan Authorities (1994)
Preparing for CCT: Specifying Housing Management, London AMA

Atkinson, J. and Elliott, L. (1994)
'Evaluation and Consumers' in Titterton, M. (ed) *Caring for People in
the Community*, London: Jessica Kingsley

Baker, R., Challen, P., Maclennan, D., Reid, V., Whitehead, C. (1992)
The Scope for Competitive Tendering of Housing Management, London:
HMSO

Birgesson, B. (1989)
'Community Care: Housing and Local Services, a Swedish Perspective',
in Kohls, M. (ed) *Making a Reality of Community Care*, Paper
presented to an International Housing Conference, Glasgow: Glasgow
DC

Catterick, P. (1992)
*Total Quality: An Introduction to Quality Management in Social
Housing*, Coventry: Institute of Housing

Cmnd 849 (1989)
Caring for People, London: HMSO

Cmnd 1599 (1991)
Citizens Charter White Paper, London: HMSO

Department of Environment (1994)
Tenant Involvement in Housing Management, London: DoE

Department of the Environment (1992)
Competing for Quality in Housing: a Consultation Paper, London: DoE

Department of the Environment (1994)
Draft Guidance: White Collar Services, London: HMSO

Housing (1993)
'Around the Table on CCT'. *Housing* Vol. 29 No. 6, pp 18–25

Inside Housing (1993)
'Tenants must be consulted on tendering', Vol. 10 No. 23, p 6

Inside Housing (1994)
'Newham won the battle, not the war', Vol. 11 No. 6, p 9

Institute of Housing (April 1993)
Housing Welfare Services and the Housing Revenue Account

Institute of Housing (1993/94)
Housing Management Standards Manual, Coventry: IoH

Karn, V., Lickiss, R., Hughes, D. and Crawley, J. (1993)
Neighbour Disputes: Responses by Social Landlords, Coventry: IoH

LGMB, AMA, ADC, ACC, COSLA (1994)
Guidance on the Assessment of Quality in the Application of CCT to White Collar and Professional Services, London: LGMB

McIntosh, A. (1993)
'Tender Moments', *Roof* Vol. 18 No. pp 38–40

Morris, H. (1994)
'Here's One He Prepared Earlier', *Inside Housing* Vol 11 No 8, pp 8–9

Pankhust, J. (1993)
'CCT – Can the comprehensive housing service survive?', *Housing and Planning Review* Vol. 48 No. 4, pp 7–10

Scottish Office (1991)
Circular on Housing and Community Care, Edinburgh: Scottish Office

Scottish Office (1992)
Competitive Tendering for Housing Management in Scotland: a consultation paper, Edinburgh: Scottish Office

Scottish Office (1994)
Community Care, a Role for Housing, Edinburgh: Scottish Office

Walsh, K. (1993)
'Contracts' in Thomas, N., Deakin, N. and Doling, J. (eds) *Learning from Innovation: Social Housing and Social Services in the 1990s*, Birmingham: Birmingham Academic Press

Walsh, K. and Spencer, K. (1990)
The Quality of Service in Housing Management, Birmingham: Institute of Local Government Studies

Watson, L. and Harker, M. (1993)
Community Care Planning: a Model for Housing Needs Assessment, London: NFHA

Welsh Office (1992)
Competing for Quality in Housing: a Consultation Paper, London: DoE